THE SPIRIT OF THOREAU

THOREAU ON LAND
Nature's Canvas

The Spirit of Thoreau

SPONSORED BY THE THOREAU SOCIETY

Wesley T. Mott, Series Editor

➤

Thoreau on Education:
Uncommon Learning

Thoreau on Science:
Material Faith

Thoreau on Mountains:
Elevating Ourselves

Thoreau on Land:
Nature's Canvas

Thoreau on Water:
Reflecting Heaven

THOREAU ON LAND

—

Nature's Canvas

Edited by J. O. Valentine

Foreword by Bill McKibben

A Mariner Original

Houghton Mifflin Company

BOSTON   NEW YORK

2001

For information about permission to reproduce selections
from this book, write to Permissions, Houghton Mifflin Company,
215 Park Avenue South, New York, New York 10003.

Visit our Web site: www.houghtonmifflinbooks.com.

Library of Congress Cataloging-in-Publication Data

Thoreau, Henry David, 1817–1862.
    Thoreau on land : nature's canvas / edited by J. O.
Valentine ; foreword by Bill McKibben.
        p. cm. — (Spirit of Thoreau)
"A Mariner original."
Includes bibliographical references.
ISBN 0-395-95385-5
    1. Nature — Literary collections.   2. Landscape —
Literary collections.   I. Valentine, J. O. (Joseph O.)
II. Thoreau, Henry David, 1817–1862. Spirit of Thoreau
series.   III. Title.
        PS3042. V27   2000
        818'.309—DC21   00-046542

Book design by Anne Chalmers
Type: Bulmer (Monotype)

Printed in the United States of America
QUM 10 9 8 7 6 5 4 3 2 1

Selections from volumes 1–5 of Thoreau's *Journal*
are from *The Writings of Henry David Thoreau*, Witherell, E., ed.
Copyright © 1972 by Princeton University Press. Reprinted
by permission of Princeton University Press.

Contents

Foreword

BILL MCKIBBEN

NATURE WRITING, broadly conceived, constitutes America's great literary gift to the world. The deepest novels, the nimblest plays, the subtlest chronicles of relations between men and women and God — all these have come from other, older traditions. But on these shores human beings came to literary consciousness before they finished subjugating the wild natural world, not long after, as in Europe and the East. And so a grand and subversive tradition of writing about the land was born, and at its source was that Concord boy Henry Thoreau.

It has always been a minority tradition, of course, at best a small corrective to the endless momentum of our urbanizing, suburbanizing, industrializing, ever-hastening Economy. But stand by Walden Pond on a bright day and count the number of people circumnavigating its shores so that they too may add a stone to the pile by the site of the old cabin. Something in his message, echoed and amplified by a thousand writers in the years since, draws us still. And that something, I suspect, is his conviction that he had located reality. That he had found a there there.

In his day, famously, no one read Thoreau, because they did not yet know their there was missing. Thoreau's feelers were so bizarrely hypersensitive that in the mild commerce of his day he could sense the approach of all the brands of alienation that now plague us. The fact that we spend most of our leisure in front of screens — TV or computer — would depress but not shock him. He wrote in 1852, to quote from a journal excerpt reprinted in this fine volume, that "if anybody thinks a thought how sure we are to hear of it — though it be only a half-thought or half a delusion it gets into newspapers and all the country rings with it." Yahoo.com indeed! By contrast, the real story of Middlesex, the timeless round of "plowing and planting and building of stone wall," went on unremarked. Except by Thoreau, who reported constantly on methods for planting peach trees, haying meadows.

Those who have read only *Walden* will come to this collection of gorgeous remnants expecting, perhaps, a sterner Thoreau than they will find. He is more patient, for instance, with farmers than he was in *Walden*. More patient in general — allowing that even a canal builder he meets, the equivalent of today's Silicon Valley entrepreneur, may have aims "as good but different" from his own. He's no less serious than in his masterwork, however. His description of the removal of a single giant pine on Fair-haven Hill (the logger has "laid waste the air. When the fish hawk in the spring revisits the banks of the Musketaquid, he will circle in vain to find his accustomed perch. . . . A plant which it has taken two centuries to perfect rising by slow stages into the heavens — has this afternoon ceased to exist") stands in just fine for the most modern accounts of Amazon deforestation. His

condemnations of the fur trader, the real estate specula-
tor, and all the rest echo just as loudly in our day.

But were he to look for small comfort in this era, he
might find it in the curious fact that he won the intellectual battle — that most of us pay at least lip service to the
value of nature. We may be congenitally unable to leave
our Palm Pilots behind and lose ourselves in a long hike,
but we mostly acknowledge that we should, and we have
set aside precisely those forests and huckleberry fields
that he envisioned as parks, and we have done it on a far
grander scale than he could have imagined. Today's
Concordians, even as they drive their SUVs and build
their mini-mansions, raise the money to restore or save
those places that meant so much to Thoreau — Walden,
Estabrook Woods, and so on.

Still, I have to believe that Thoreau would be pressing
his neighbors harder, urging them to think of the architecture of their entire lives. For of course the nature writing that he helped found is only half about nature. Our
own nature is the other half of the relationship, the
harder half. And ultimately it is our realness that
Thoreau yearns for — a solidity based on something
more than economy or government. He aims for the
heart, and he hits it more often than any other writer this
nation has yet produced. He cannot be read by an honest
American without the constant twinge of recognition,
and the at least sporadic resolve to change our ways. He
stands on firmer ground, more solid land, than currently
exists.

Let Men Lead Manly,
Independent Lives

As if at once to publicly declare his own philosophy and chart a course for the remainder of his life, David Henry Thoreau, when he addressed the gathering of classmates and honored guests assembled at his Harvard commencement, said, "Let men, true to their natures, cultivate the moral affections, lead manly and independent lives" (E. W. Emerson, 19). And then, with a flourish —perhaps to make his convictions seem more real—he rearranged his name to read "Henry David Thoreau" and set out to abide by those words.

Thoreau's life, however, turned out to be anything but well charted, its course, never straight and true. Like the Concord landscape he would come to adore, his was a life filled with contrasts and contradictions.

It was true he possessed an independent spirit, but other aspects of his personality are not so easily characterized. He was a moralist and an intellectual, a thinker, philosopher, poet, and reformer. However, he seemed to be most comfortable in the presence of the common man. He was a native New Englander—a solid Yankee; an American, during a time when this country was trying desperately to define its own identity. Still, he was never blindly obedient to civil authority and often railed against bondage, injustice, and the American system of politics in general. And although he is most often portrayed as a recluse, a rustic oddity, he also knew the importance of society. "There are two worlds — the post office & Nature — I know them both," he once said (3 January 1853, *Journal*).

He enjoyed the discovery of new things and, even more, liked telling people about them — especially if the encounter included some verbal sparring and *he* came away knowing something new as well. Yet he was also content to keep the knowledge of some newly discovered plant or animal specimen a secret, to be shared only with his journal. Indeed, for years he filled notebook after notebook with quotations and facts concerning the American Indian, without, as far as we know, ever making the purpose of his notations clear to anyone.

He was said to be both a cantankerous and a serious man, who was known to have frequented the "Valley of Sorrow" (E. W. Emerson, 27). But he also made music, created toys, and played games with children. He was soulful and passionate about many things in his life, yet was never able to form a romantic relationship. He devoted much space in his journal to scathing attacks on business, the state of commerce in the world, and the daily toil and drudgery that so many of his Concord neighbors seemed to endure as they endeavored to earn their livelihoods. Yet even a cursory reading of his journal, a record of his life over a twenty-four-year period that grew to more than two million words, shows that he obviously toiled over his own endeavors, spending his entire life trying to establish a career as a writer — and make it pay.

However, one common thread ran through this fabric of inconsistency, this life of contrasts — one true and unchanging rule that governed most of his behavior throughout his years: his abiding love for nature and the land. He said: "I love nature. I love the landscape because it is so sincere. It never cheats me. It never jests — It is cheerfully — musically earnest. I relie on the earth" (16 November 1850, *Journal*).

The origins of this affection for nature and the land are difficult to determine. At the time of Thoreau's graduation from Harvard, in 1837, his ideas about man and his relationship to the natural world largely mirrored those of his Concord neighbor Ralph Waldo Emerson, to whom he had not yet been formally introduced.

Thoreau's mother once proudly exclaimed, "How much Mr. Emerson does talk like my Henry" (Baker, 109). However, as Emerson was quick to recognize, there was a certain singularity and originality of thought in this most gifted son of a working-class Concord family. He seems to have "as free and erect a mind as any I have ever met," Emerson said in 1838, not long after Thoreau's graduation (R. W. Emerson, *Journals,* 11 February 1838). Moreover, the primordial source of Thoreau's intellectual talent was fascinating to Emerson, particularly that such a fine mind could spring from such modest family beginnings.

Thoreau was born on 12 July 1817 in the easternmost upper chamber of a gray, unpainted saltbox on Virginia Road, the oldest byway into Concord. He was the son of

Cynthia and John Thoreau, and it was fitting that his birthplace was a farmer's home, with a rear lean-to that hugged the earth and an architecture that, to Thoreau, gave the appearance of a house seated on its haunches, "bearing the sky on its broad shoulders like Atlas" (Blanding, 12). His birthplace, one of the oldest inland farms in America, stood on land that once belonged to the Wheelers and the Minots. His friend and first biographer, William Ellery Channing, said, "It was lovely he should draw his first breath in pure country, out of the crowded towns, amid the pleasant russet fields" (Channing, 1–2).

Even at an early age, Henry seemed to possess a certain "spirituality," or depth of understanding, that did not go without notice. It is told that he would often lie awake at night, long after his brother John had fallen asleep in the small bed they shared. One night, finding Henry awake even longer than usual, his mother asked why he wasn't yet asleep. He replied, "Mother, I have been looking through the stars to see if I couldn't see God behind them" (E. W. Emerson, 15).

Both of Thoreau's parents enjoyed the outdoors, and they would take "nature walks" in the woods and along the shores of the river, streams, and ponds. H. S. Canby, an early-twentieth-century biographer of Thoreau, said, "Gossip reported that, thanks to an ill-timed excursion, one of [Cynthia Thoreau's] children was nearly born on Lee's Hill" (Canby, 20). Some of Thoreau's earliest impressions were those of being immersed in nature. For example, writing in his journal from his cabin along the shores of Walden Pond in 1845, he remembers vividly his earliest visit to Walden at age five:

Twenty-three years since, when I was five years old, I was brought from Boston to this pond, away in the country,—which was then but another name for the extended world for me,—one of the most ancient scenes stamped on the tablets of my memory, the oriental Asiatic valley of my world, whence so many races and inventions have gone forth in recent times. That woodland vision for a long time made the drapery of my dreams. That sweet solitude my spirit seemed so early to require that I might have room to entertain my thronging guests, and that speaking silence that my ears might distinguish the significant sounds. Somehow or other it at once gave the preference to this recess among the pines, where almost sunshine and shadow were the only inhabitants that varied the scene, over that tumultuous and varied city, as if it had found its proper nursery (August 1845, *Journal*).

Tahatawan's Musketaquid

During his "growing years," Thoreau became a child of the woods. Although most of his outdoor activities differed little from those of other New England boys of his time—shooting, fishing, swimming—there was early evidence of a tendency to want to be alone, to shun social gatherings and, instead, cultivate his own more solitary interests. As a young adult, however, he relished the company of his older brother as a fellow "traveller" through the landscape. Along with John, Henry would develop what was to be a lifelong interest in Native Americans, their understanding of the ways of nature, and their relationship with the land. In a spirited and playful style, the two brothers would sometimes communicate with each other in the period's clichéd imitation of Indian speech. In 1837 he wrote to John:

> Brother, it is many suns that I have not seen the print of thy moccasins by our council fire, the Great Spirit has blown more leaves from the trees and many clouds from the land of snows have visited our lodge — the earth has become hard like a frozen buffalo skin, so that the trampling of many herds is like the Great Spirit's thunder — the grass on the great fields is like the old man of eighty winters — and the small song-sparrow prepares for his flight to the land whence the summer comes (*Correspondence*, 16).

He signed these letters "Tahatawan," whom he believed was the old Sachem of Musketaquid ("the place where the water flows through grasses"), and made the mark of a bow and arrow.

Thoreau was devastated when John died of lockjaw in 1842. The Indian "games" that the two brothers had enjoyed together would form the basis for his later pursuit of trying to understand the history and legacy of America's native people.

Even much later in his life, Thoreau never ceased to be amazed when, often unexpectedly, the soil would seem to regurgitate some ancient relic — especially if the artifact was an Indian arrowhead, which to him represented "humanity inscribed on the face of the earth" (28 March 1859, *Journal*). But as he grew intellectually, his interest in the American Indian evolved from a focus chiefly on collecting unusual artifacts to more serious scholarly research, whereby he sought to move beyond conventional nineteenth-century assumptions about the Indian toward a deeper insight into their culture. And for Thoreau, there was little about Native Americans that could surpass his interest in their spiritual relationship with the land they inhabited. For they were the earlier stewards of his Holy Land, his Concord, his native soil — a holy land where he would go to worship nature through daily excursions that would themselves become crusades.

The Land Is Alive

To Thoreau, "land" meant more than mere soil. Nor was it simply *real* estate. For him, land was the equivalent of a living organism. In fact, he believed the whole earth was alive: "Even the solid globe is permeated by the living law. It is the most living of creatures. No doubt all creatures that live on its surface are but parasites" (31 December 1851, *Journal*).

Further, the living earth, and the creatures that live on its surface, made up only a portion of what he so often referred to as the "natural landscape." According to Thoreau's view, the complete, modern natural landscape had to include man and the "sky above his head." He once remarked, "How little matters it all they have built and delved there in the valley — it is after all but a feature in the landscape" (transcribed 1842, *Journal*). And that landscape, by virtue of man's presence there, must also necessarily include his inventions — cities, ships, roads and railroads, telegraphs and churches.

It is clear from reading Thoreau's journal passages that he took genuine pleasure from what were to become "spiritual" encounters with the land. He enjoyed exploring new features of the landscape he had never seen before. It made no difference if they were to be found on the top of a mountain or buried beneath the muck of a swamp. He welcomed the landscape by moonlight or at high noon, in sunlight or in a fog, from a hill or a valley, examined up close or seen from a distance through a looking glass, in rain or snow, from his boat on the river or standing knee deep in the grasses of a meadow — and even from an inverted position, upside down with his head bent between his knees. He was always impressed by the vastness of nature and by the visual contrasts and enormous diversity of elements in the landscape, which to him all seemed to play together with the sweetest of harmony. "Our country is broad and rich," he said (20 December 1851, *Journal*). The author and editor Paul Brooks once commented, "In all American literature there is no writer so directly, so fiercely concerned, not simply with the abstract concept of nature, but with the living land itself" (Gleason, Introduction).

Despite all that has been said over time about Thoreau's enchantment with nature and the land and his important contributions as a naturalist, it is important to remember that he was, first and always, a writer, one who worked diligently at his craft. In addition to the delight and inspiration he felt when perhaps viewing a beautiful sunset from a favorite hillside haunt, at least some of the pleasure he derived from the experience surely had to do with his wonderful gift of being able to convey all of the detail, richness, and sensuality of that vision with simply a pen and a piece of paper.

In his earlier years, Thoreau's power as a writer came from his ability to identify spiritually with his natural surroundings. To him, wildness was indeed a tonic, an elixir for the soul: "You must converse much with the field and woods if you would imbibe such health into your mind and spirit as you covet for your body" (31 December 1841, *Journal*). And nature was a mere reflection of man's inner spiritual life: "A lake is the landscape's most beautiful and expressive feature. It is earth's eye; looking into which the beholder measures the depth of his own nature" (*Walden*, 186).

However, as Robert Finch has accurately pointed out, over the years, as Thoreau was exposed to a greater variety of literature and art, his landscape descriptions began to exhibit less of the "Romantic impulse to see nature as a reflection and measure of the observer's spiritual life" (Rothwell, Introduction) and included more of the techniques of field observation and scientific analysis. This change in style has been noted by others as well (see, for example, Krutch, 1948; Harding, 1959). This is not a surprising development in the evolution of Thoreau's style of writing, considering what events were occurring in areas of natural science in this country as well as in other parts of the world during the middle of the nineteenth century — most especially, Darwin's observations on natural selection. Certainly, such revolutionary thought had an effect on Thoreau's method and expressive style of portraying the landscape. In fact, as Finch says, increasingly Thoreau used "himself as a measure of nature," describing less and less how it *acted* on his own spirit, or inner psyche, and more in terms of how his own body *reacted* to its effects. For example, he used his body to gauge the strength of the wind or drenched "himself in storms to measure their force."

Regardless of this evolution from a Romantic to a more "observational" style, Thoreau's later descriptions of the New England landscape never lacked passion and remain some of the richest, most inspiring ever written. Because he seldom left Concord, he visited certain locations over and over and thus became keenly aware of even the subtlest change in the landscape wrought by time. This sensitivity gives him a powerful advantage over other nature writers. In a sense, he was like an accomplished musician who, over the course of many years, has worked again and again with a certain complex piece of music until he no longer hears the individual notes—only the complete song. Thoreau's pen was his instrument and Concord became his song. He never tired of describing the same natural scenes because, as he said, "with each new visit I am different." Wendell Berry, in talking about his own development as a writer and the importance that an intimate knowledge of one's own landscape can assume, eloquently expresses this connection between writing and place in the following way: "This place has become the form of my work, its discipline, in the same way the sonnet has been the form and discipline of the work of other poets: if it doesn't fit it's not true" (Berry, 92).

Concord's Own Evolution

In the mid-1800s, about the time Thoreau's written portraits of the landscape were changing, Concord was undergoing its own evolution right under his feet. During the years of Henry Thoreau's youth, Concord, like most New England settlements, was an agrarian community. But Concord was never a small village, by New England standards. Comprising an area of thirty-six square miles, by the time of Thoreau's graduation from Harvard it boasted two thousand inhabitants. It was a major crossroads, connecting Watertown and Boston to the east with the Berkshires to the west, and the New Hampshire hill country to the north with Sudbury and southern New England to the south. It was a busy place, often filled with travelers and the wagon traffic of teamsters passing through on their way to destinations at all points on the compass.

Whereas the original settlers of the town found open land only in the water meadows and bogs, the rest being heavily forested, by the early 1800s farmers with oxen had already succeeded in stripping the landscape of trees and rooting out all the stumps. They constructed neat and tidy walls to border their properties, built from the granite rocks strewn above and below the surface of their newly cleared fields, which they swore were the Lord's joke—put there purposely to crack plowshares. The result of this intensive clearing was that only about 11 percent of the land remained wooded. Except for the area right around the milldam, the hub of the village, pastures, meadows, and tilled fields made up most of the Concord landscape. In 1820, 262 Concord men were engaged in agriculture. Compared to the New England landscape of today, with its many wooded acres, it is hard to imagine what Concord's surrounding countryside must have looked like to Thoreau. With so few trees, the pastoral scene one could enjoy from even the slightest elevation was one of gently rolling green pastures, meadows, and bogs, dotted with the dark-brown tilled earth of the small farms and the few remaining woodlots, each not more than several acres in size. Even in the early 1840s, during what Van Wyck Brooks has called the intellectual "flowering of New England," agriculture remained strong in Concord. As the agricultural historian Wayne Rasmussen has pointed out, these years represented "the golden age when Concord was supplying food to Boston and ideas to the world" (*Concord Journal,* 25 April 1996, 10).

Thoreau's relationship with the Concord husbandman of the period has always been a matter of dispute. The perception persists to this day that he held farmers in low regard. In 1939 Canby explained this supposed lack of esteem in the following way:

> There was a social difference between "farmers" and "townsmen" which was occupational. The farmers dressed and lived and thought differently. Thoreau, of course, was a townsman in spite of his woodcraft. He liked farmers, but did not altogether approve of them, because their brains were conditioned by the oxen they worked in the fields. (Canby, 10–11)

That the ox could have such an effect on the farmer was Thoreau's idea, not Canby's. In his journal, Thoreau said that the farmer was "ox-like in his thought, in his walk, in his strength, in his trustworthiness, in his taste" (4 September 1851, *Journal*). However, it is more likely that the source of this observation was Thoreau's preconceptions of what constituted the ideal, simple, rural lifestyle rather than any particular contempt for farmers or the occupation of farming.

Even though determined to avoid "old set ways" and to follow a path through life without falling into preexisting ruts, Thoreau's own experiment in living at Walden

—and a history of some unrewarding encounters with both individuals and entire groups of people along the way—shattered some of his ideas about what constituted a higher, or spiritual, life. Although an advocate for simple living, he discovered that a primitive, "savage" lifestyle, lived in relative poverty, was not necessarily conducive to elevated thinking. Many of his prior assumptions—for example, about the noble, savage Indian living in complete spiritual harmony with nature and the land—were not confirmed once he confronted reality. This happened on his 1846 trip to the Maine woods, when he met some Indians whom he described as "sinister and slouching fellows," and then went on to note in his journal that the history of the red man is "a history of fixed habits of stagnation" (23 January 1858, *Journal*). Even in his own backyard, his prior opinions were shaken when he was exposed to Irish immigrants like John Field, who lived with his wife and children in a filthy small hut with chickens "like members of the family" roaming through the makeshift dwelling, and who could not see that there was any better way of living; the end result being that when John Field changed seats, "luck changed seats too" (23 August 1845, *Journal*). Or, in his encounters with Alek Therien, the woodchopper, who first appeared to lead a joyful, self-sufficient, and simple life but ended up being a source of frustration because Thoreau could never, "by any maneuvering, ... get him to take the spiritual view of things" (29 December 1853, *Journal*). These and other similar experiences came as a blow to Thoreau's transcendental belief that all men possess the dormant seed of spirituality, which— buried just below the surface of a rough, element-worn exterior — simply waits for the proper environment and careful nurturing in order to flourish (Shi, 146–48). Consequently, he came to feel more and more that some men were destined to live their lives like serfs, that in some men neither worldly instruction nor even the acts of the gods could induce any form of intellectual curiosity, moral sense, or self-worth. Although he placed some farmers in this category, he did not consider an individual's unwillingness to rise to a higher and more ethereal plane to be an occupational hazard — say, because farmers had their brains conditioned by oxen — but, rather, an immutable trait in each person's character.

On many occasions, Thoreau expressed admiration for the hard physical labor of the farmer and for the beauty of the agricultural landscape. And, as if he never wanted to give up entirely the strong elements of hope and optimism in his original ideas of Transcendentalism, his journal is filled with descriptions of those "men of the soil" — like George Minot and Edmund Hosmer — who most closely resembled his ideal farmer: learned and cultured, living simply and self-sufficiently, making "the most of his labor," and doing "nothing with haste and drudgery, but as if he loved it" (4 October 1851, *Journal*).

In 1844, the Boston–Fitchburg railroad line reached Concord. Now competing with the sound of the meeting-house bell that for generations had regulated town life was the new sound of the steam whistle, which signaled profound changes for the citizens of this rural village. Thoreau continued to seek refuge in the countryside. One of his favorite haunts was what he called the Easterbrooks Country, today known as Estabrook Woods, and another was the wooded area around Walden Pond. The new railroad cut right through

Walden Woods, just skirting the southwest corner of the pond. In what was probably the first shot fired in the still ongoing battle to protect Walden Woods, the citizens of Concord expressed their distress at this disruption of the beauty and serenity of what at the time was one of the few remaining tracts of woodland in the town. As Paul Brooks recounts in *The People of Concord* (112), while the railroad was "still being built, many of the town's most distinguished men and women, beginning with Emerson and Alcott, addressed a petition to the railroad's general manager:

> 'We citizens of Concord respectfully and urgently remind you that your contractors are now building the new line through what is to us and to all lovers of nature most precious ground. The No. branch of Concord river is our Central Park and one of the most beautiful pieces of simple scenery in New England. We feel it is bad enough to have a railroad at all in that place, but the ruthless destruction of a single tree, or shrub, for fire wood or for any purpose not absolutely necessary to building the road will be viewed by us all as barbarism which we hope you can and will prevent.'

Thoreau, however, remained optimistic about the event and in several journal entries expressed his delight and interest in everything about the railroad, from the rattling of the cars to the interesting sand beneath the tracks. For example: "The r-road is perhaps our pleasantest & wildest road. It only makes deep cuts into & through the hills — on it are no houses nor foot travellers. The travel on it does not disturb me. The woods are left to hang over it" (9 March 1852, *Journal*).

This assessment of what clearly was viewed as an environmental intrusion by other "prominent" Concord citizens might leave the committed "radical" environmentalist of today somewhat confused about where Thoreau, long considered to be a father of the conservation movement in America, actually stood. In 1851, the telegraph came to Concord, and Thoreau once again perceived the event with characteristic wide-eyed enthusiasm, likening the telegraph wires to a vibrating harp and commenting that "the telegraph harp has spoken to me more distinctly and effectually than any man ever did" (15 March 1852, *Journal*).

Thoreau adopted what would be considered today a moderate view on issues related to the introduction of new technology and the conservation of natural sites. His was more of an all-encompassing view of nature that included in it a role for man, a view that was accepting of new features in the landscape, both natural and artificial. He was reluctant to let those speak for nature who had little or no direct contact or experience with her, and valued the opinions of even the most "savage" woodsmen over scholars crying out to protect something with which they were plainly unfamiliar. He said, "The surliness with which the wood-chopper speaks of his woods, handling them as indifferently as his axe, is better than the mealy-mouthed enthusiasm of the lover of nature" (*A Week on the Concord and Merrimack Rivers,* 108–9).

Eventually, however, both the railroad and the telegraph brought about changes in Concord that moved Thoreau himself to stand and "speak a word for nature." The railroad effectively reduced travel time to Boston, a four-hour coach ride, to less than an hour. The "cars" brought competition to the local farmers and took away their sons and daughters. Small family subsistence farms gave way to larger market-driven farms, and some of these, especially dairy farms, which could now sell their milk and dairy products to Bostonians, were successful. Gradually, however, many of the small homesteads, without a new generation of farmers to run them, began to collapse and disappear. Concord agriculture was undergoing a revolution. Older farmers, stunned by the changing requirements of a way of life that had carried their ancestors for generations, knew no other way to live. Many soon fell into conditions of deep poverty and really did end up leading the "lives of quiet desperation" that Thoreau so often criticized.

Moreover, the tracks of the railroad provided the villagers a straight and narrow path to wider horizons. Concord citizens who normally never would have traveled much beyond the Cambridge Turnpike could now feed the chickens in the morning, spend the day experiencing the thrills of city life in Boston, and return home in time to milk the cow in the evening. Their lives were changing. They now expected more.

But it was the changing concept of land ownership and the destruction of the woodlands that seemed to raise Thoreau's hackles. Even though during the early 1840s there was a growing interest among intellectuals in exploring the possibilities of communal living, as evidenced by utopian ventures such as the founding of Brook Farm in West Roxbury in 1841, and Bronson Alcott's Fruitlands in 1843, during the 1850s general attitudes about land ownership were shifting in the opposite direction, favoring speculation in land values by individuals, and the prohibition of theretofore traditional activities on privately owned property. Common lands slowly disappeared and fences were erected where they hadn't existed before, cramping the perambulatory style of "cross-lot" walkers like Thoreau. In addition, the railroad brought more industry and commerce to Concord: first ice harvesting on Walden Pond and then gunpowder and woolen mills. The requirement of lumber for new buildings put additional stresses on the already depleted woodlands of the town. Though parlor stoves and cookstoves began to replace the open hearth for cooking and heating during Thoreau's time, inventory takers recorded few stoves in *farmers'* houses in Massachusetts until well after 1840 (Larkin, 141). Thus, there continued to be a high demand for wood. A frugal Concord farmer could get by on about six cords of wood per year; an average household, on twenty; and a well-paid minister like Ezra Ripley, on the thirty cords that was part of his salary. The city of Boston put even more strains on the woodlands of rural towns like Concord and was already tapping the forests of Maine for the six hundred thousand cords it required annually (Richardson, 16). Demand far exceeded supply. The sound of the woodsman's ax was heard everywhere.

Thoreau responded to this onslaught by trying to emphasize the spiritual qualities of these rapidly disappearing natural sanctuaries. Yet, during his lifetime, his many pleas for a saner world were barely heard beyond the confines of his own study. His journal articles and field notebooks rarely saw the light of day, except to accompany him on his walks; and his books were never widely read nor well accepted. As a man in his forties, he had no illusions about the impact he was making on his fellow man.

In his essay "Walking" he wrote the now famous sentence "In wildness is the preservation of the world." However, Thoreau came to believe that, although wildness was essential to a moral awakening and spiritual health, one could best soar to higher heights through regular *visitations* with nature, coupled with a steady mixture of culture, learning, and society. Increasingly, he grew more accepting of the village and its inhabitants, viewing them as an integral and necessary part of his Concord landscape. At times he even seemed to take some measure of enjoyment in listening to the "hum" of the townspeople as they sat "forever in public avenues without stirring," letting all the latest news "simmer and whisper through them like the Etesian winds" (*Walden*, 167). The truth was that he needed both his solitude and his society. He appreciated the delicate inverse relationship between the two. He knew that the unchecked growth of one could mean the slow death of the other. The path to his Elysian Fields cut through both village and wilderness, and as long as the two were in balance, it could be a good walk.

For so long, Thoreau was seen by his neighbors as a solitary figure set against the backdrop of the Concord landscape, not unlike the cut-out paper silhouettes that adorned the walls of many of their homes. He seemed a pleasant enough but somewhat standoffish character who was not inclined to social intercourse and apparently lacked the ability to develop any deep and lasting bonds of friendship with his contemporary villagers. Yet Thoreau himself grew to understand that he needed these village people as desperately as he needed his nature and his native land. It is somewhat symbolic, somewhat telling, given the course of his short life of forty-four years, that in Thoreau's first entry in his journal he sought solitude:

> To be alone I find it necessary to escape the present, —I avoid myself. How could I be alone in the Roman Emperor's chamber of mirrors? I seek a garret (22 October 1837, *Journal*).

Twenty-four years later—still ill with tuberculosis after returning from a convalescent trip to Minnesota and knowing he would soon die—in a communication to his friend Daniel Ricketson (*Correspondence,* 625)—he sought friendship and society:

> Remembering your numerous invitations, I write this short note now chiefly to say that, if you are to be at home, and it will be quite agreeable to you, I will pay you a visit next week, & take such rides or sauntering walks with you as an invalid may.
>
> Yrs
> Henry D. Thoreau

Thoreau on Land

Musketaquid: Thoreau's Native American Landscape

Today, in our time of ecological crisis, people turn to the writings of Henry Thoreau and the speeches and prophecies of great Indian chiefs as if they give a common spiritual support. The words of Thoreau and the warnings of Black Elk, Chief Joseph, or Chief Seattle—showing up on fund-raising leaflets, on posters, and in luxurious picture books—seem almost interchangeable. And despite repetition and inappropriate surroundings, the words move us. They seem to come from Nature and an unviolated Past, speaking for the Land and the Animals and those generations which modern man forgets, those Ahead. Thoreau, that most thoroughly naturalized American, is at one with the great chiefs. Together, he and they are our modern admonitors.

— Robert F. Sayre

A Vanished Race

When I walk in the fields of Concord and meditate on the destiny of this prosperous slip of the Saxon *family*—the unexhausted energies of this new country—I forget that this which is now Concord was once Musketaquid and that the *American race* has had its destiny also. Everywhere in the fields—in the corn and grain land—the earth is strewn with the relics of a race which has vanished as completely as if trodden in with the earth.

19 March 1842, Journal 1: 380

Indian Graves

There might be seen here on the bank of the Merrimack, near Goff's Falls, in what is now the town of Bedford, famous "for hops and for its fine domestic manufactures," some graves of the aborigines. The land still bears this scar here, and time is slowly crumbling the bones of a race. Yet without fail every spring since they first fished and hunted here, the brown thrasher has heralded the morning from a birch or alder spray, and the undying race of reed-birds still rustles through the withering grass. But these bones rustle not. These mouldering elements are slowly preparing for another metamorphosis, to serve new masters, and what was the Indian's will ere long be the white man's sinew.

"Wednesday," *A Week on the Concord and Merrimack Rivers*, 237

Indian Fishing Grounds

We saw near the river, where the sand was blown off down to some ancient surface, the foundation of an Indian wigwam exposed, a perfect circle of burnt stones four or five feet in diameter, mingled with fine charcoal and the bones of small animals, which had been preserved in the sand. The surrounding sand was sprinkled with other burnt stones on which their fires had been built, as well as with flakes of arrow-head stone, and we found one perfect arrow-head. In one place we noted where an Indian had sat to manufacture arrow-heads out of quartz, and the sand was sprinkled with a quart of small glass-like chips about as big as a fourpence, which he had broken off in his work. Here, then, the Indians must have fished before the whites arrived.

"Monday," *A Week on the Concord
and Merrimack Rivers*, 146–47

Discovering New Faculties

Having returned, I flatter myself that the world appears in some respects a little larger, and not, as usual, smaller and shallower, for having extended my range. I have made a shore excursion into the new world which the Indian dwells in, or is. He begins where we leave off. It is worth the while to detect new faculties in man, — he is so much the more divine; and anything that fairly excites our admiration expands us. The Indian, who can find his way so wonderfully in the woods, possesses so much intelligence which the white man does not, —and it increases my own capacity, as well as faith, to observe it. I rejoice to find that intelligence flows in other channels than I knew. It redeems for me portions of what seemed brutish before.

18 August 1857, Letter to H. G. O. Blake,
Correspondence, 491–92

Where Is This Country?

What a new aspect have new eyes given to the land. Where is this country but in the hearts of its inhabitants why there is only so much of Indian America left—as there is of the American Indian in the character of this generation.

19 March 1842, *Journal* 1: 382

The Arrowhead

A curious incident happened some four or six weeks ago which I think it worth the while to record. John and I had been searching for Indian relics, and been successful enough to find two arrowheads and a pestle, when, of a Sunday evening, with our heads full of the past and its remains, we strolled to the mouth of Swamp-bridge brook. As we neared the brow of the hill forming the bank of the river, inspired by my theme, I broke forth into an extravagant eulogy on those savage times, using most violent gesticulations by way of illustration.

"There on Nawshawtuct," said I, "was their lodge, the rendezvous of the tribe, and yonder, on Clamshell hill their feasting ground. This was no doubt a favorite haunt; here on this brow was an eligible look-out post. How often have they stood on this very spot, at this very hour, when the sun was sinking behind yonder woods, and gilding with his last rays the waters of the Musketaquid, and pondered the days success and the morow's prospects, or communed with the spirits of their fathers gone before them, to the land of shades!—"Here," I exclaimed, "stood Tahatawan; and there, (to complete the period,) is Tahatawan's arrowhead"

We instantly proceeded to sit down on the spot I had pointed to, and I, to carry out the joke, to lay bare an ordinary stone, which my whim had selected, when lo! the first I laid hands on, the grubbing stone that was to be, proved a most perfect arrowhead, as sharp as if just from the hands of the Indian fabricator!!!

29 October 1837, *Journal* 1: 8–9

Indian Corn Hills

Went through the old cornfield on the hill side beyond now grown up to birches & hickories. Woods where you feel the old corn hills under your feet — for these not being disturbed or levelled in getting the crop like potatoe hills last an indefinite while — & by some they are called Indian corn fields — though I think erroniously not only from their position in rock soil frequently — but because the squaws probably with their clam shells or thin stones or wooden hoes did not hill their corn more than many now recommend.

12 September 1851, *Journal* 4: 79

Indian Blood

I love that the rocks should appear to have some spots of blood on them. Indian blood at least — to be convinced that the earth has been crowded with men — living enjoying suffering — that races past away have stained the rocks with their blood — That the mould I tread on has been animated — aye humanized. I am the more at home. I farm the dust of my ancestors — though the chemists analysis may not detect it — I go forth to redeem the meadows they have become.

4 March 1852, *Journal* 4: 375–76

Last Services for Her Race

The names of those who bought these fields of the Red men the wild men of the woods — are Buttrick Davis Barrett Bulkley &c &c v Hist. Here and there still you will find a man with Indian blood in his veins. An eccentric farmer descended from an Indian Chief — Or you will see a solitary pure blooded Indian looking as wild as ever among the pines — one of the last of the massachusett's tribes stepping into a railroad car with his gun & pappoose

Still here and there an Indian squaw with her dog — her only companion — lives in some lone house — insulted by school children — making baskets & picking berries her employment You will meet her on the highway — with few children or none — with melancholy face — history destiny — stepping after her race — who had stayed to tuck them up in their long sleep. For whom berries condescend to grow. I have not seen one on the Musketaquid for many a year And some who came up in their canoes and camped on its banks a dozen years ago had to ask me where it came from. A lone Indian woman without children — acompanied by her dog — weaving the shroud of her race — performing the last services for her departed race. Not yet absorbed into the elements again — A daughter of the soil — one of the nobility of the land — the white man an imported weed burdock & mullein which displace the ground nut.

After 16 July 1850, *Journal* 3: 93

Indian Store Holes

Amoskeag, or Namaskeak, is said to mean "great fishing place." It was hereabouts that the Sachem Wannalancet resided. Tradition says that his tribe, when at war with the Mohawks, concealed their provisions in the cavities of the rocks in the upper part of these falls. The Indians who hid their provisions in these holes, and affirmed "that God had cut them out for that purpose," understood their origin and use better than the Royal Society, who in their Transactions, in the last century, speaking of

these very holes, declare that "they seem plainly to be artificial."

"Wednesday," *A Week on the Concord
and Merrimack Rivers*, 246

So Old, So Young

It was in fact an old battle and hunting ground through
which we had been floating, the ancient dwelling-place of
a race of hunters and warriors. Their weirs of stone, their
arrowheads and hatchets, their pestles, and the mortars
in which they pounded Indian corn before the white man
had tasted it, lay concealed in the mud of the river bottom. Tradition still points out the spots where they took
fish in the greatest numbers, by such arts as they possessed. It is a rapid story the historian will have to put together. Miantonimo, — Winthrop, — Webster. Soon he
comes from Mount Hope to Bunker Hill, from bearskins,
parched corn, bows and arrows, to tiled roofs, wheat
fields, guns and swords. Pawtucket and Wamesit, where
the Indians resorted in the fishing season, are now Lowell, the city of spindles and Manchester of America,
which sends its cotton cloth round the globe. Even we
youthful voyagers had spent a part of our lives in the village of Chelmsford, when the present city, whose bells we
heard, was its obscure north district only, and the giant
weaver was not yet fairly born. So old are we; so young is
it.

"Sunday," *A Week on the Concord
and Merrimack Rivers*, 82–83

Civilized Indians

We talk of civilizing the Indian, but that is not the name
for his improvement. By the wary independence and

aloofness of his dim forest life he preserves his intercourse with his native gods, and is admitted from time to
time to a rare and peculiar society with nature.

"Sunday," *A Week on the Concord
and Merrimack Rivers*, 55

The Indian's Compass

These are interesting groves of young soft white pines 18
feet high — whose vigorous yellowish green shoots of this
season from 3 to 18 inches long at the extremities of all
the branches contrast remarkably with the dark green of
the old leaves. I observe that these shoots are bent and
what is more remarkable all one way i.e. to the east — almost at a right angle the topmost ones —

and I am reminded of the observation in Henry's Adventures that the Indians guided themselves in cloudy
weather by this mark — All these shoots excepting those
low down on the East side are bent toward the east. I am
very much pleased with this observation confirming that
of the Indians. I was singularly impressed when I first observed that all the young pines in this pasture obeyed this
law — without regard to the direction of the wind or the
shelter of other trees. To make myself more sure of the direction — as it was not easy to determine it exactly standing on one side where so many shoots were bent in the
air — I went behind the trees on the W. till the bent shoot
appeared as a straight line — & then by observing my
shadow & guessing at the time of day I decided that their

direction was due east. This gives me more satisfaction than any observation I have made for a long time. This is true of the rapidly growing shoots. How long will this phenomenon avail to guide the traveller? How soon do they become erect? A natural compass. How few civilised men probably have ever made this observation—so important to the savage! How much may there have been known to his woodcraft—which has not been detected by science!

23 June 1852, Journal 5: 128–29

A Song for the Indian

Sat under the dark hemlocks—gloomy hemlocks on the hill-side beyond. In a stormy day like this there is the gloom of night beneath them. The ground beneath them almost bare with wet rocks & fine twigs—without leaves (but hemlock leaves) or grass. The birds are singing in the rain about the small pond in front— The inquisitive chicadee that has flown at once to the alders to reconnoitre as the black birds—the song-sparrow telling of expanding buds. But above all the robin sings here too— I know not at what distance in the wood. Did he sing thus in Indian days?, I ask myself—for I have always associated this sound with the village & the clearing, but now I do detect the aboriginal wildness in his strain—& can imagine him a woodland bird—and that he sang thus when there was no civilized ear to hear him—a pure forest melody even like the wood thrush. Every genuine thing retains this wild tone—which no true culture displaces—I heard him even as he might have sounded to the Indian singing at evening upon the elm above his wigwam—with which was associated in the red-man's mind the events of an Indian's life.— his childhood. Formerly I had heard in it only those strains which tell of the white man's village life — now I heard those strains which remembered the red man's life — such as fell on the ears of Indian children. — as he sang when these arrow-heads which the rain has made shine so on the lean stubble field — were fastened to their shaft.

21 April 1852, Journal 4: 479

Yankees

The white man comes, pale as the dawn, with a load of thought, with a slumbering intelligence as a fire raked up, knowing well what he knows, not guessing but calculating; strong in community, yielding obedience to authority; of experienced race; of wonderful, wonderful common sense; dull but capable, slow but persevering, severe but just, of little humor but genuine; a laboring man, despising game and sport; building a house that endures, a framed house. He buys the Indian's moccasins and baskets, then buys his hunting grounds, and at length forgets where he is buried, and plows up his bones. And here town records, old, tattered, time-worn, weather-stained chronicles, contain the Indian sachem's mark, perchance, an arrow or a beaver, and the few fatal words by which he deeded his hunting grounds away. He comes with a list of ancient Saxon, Norman, and Celtic names, and strews them up and down this river, — Framingham, Sudbury, Bedford, Carlisle, Billerica, Chelmsford, — and this is New Angle-land, and these are the new West Saxons, whom the Red Men call, not Angle-ish or English, but Yengeese, and so at last they are known for Yankees.

"Sunday," A Week on the Concord
and Merrimack Rivers, 53

One Beautiful Country

Bangor to Oldtown May 10th — The rail-roa
gor to Oldtown is civilization shooting off
into the forest. — I had much conversatior
Indian at the latter place, who sat dreaming up..
at the water side — and striking his deer-skin moccasins
against the planks — while his arms hung listlessly by his
side. He was the most communicative man I had met. —
Talked of hunting and fishing — old times and new times.
Pointing up the Penobscot he observed — "Two or three
miles up the river one beautiful country!" And then as if
he would come as far to meet me as I had gone to meet
him — he exclaimed — "Ugh! one very hard time!" But he
had mistaken his man.

10 May 1838, *Journal* 1: 46

A Revolution of Nature

The revolutions of nature tell as fine tales, and make as
interesting revelations, on this river's banks, as on the
Euphrates or the Nile. This apple-tree, which stands
within a few rods of the river, is called "Elisha's apple-
tree," from a friendly Indian, who was anciently in the
service of Jonathan Tyng, and, with one other man, was
killed here by his own race in one of the Indian wars, —
the particulars of which affair were told us on the spot.
He was buried close by, no one knew exactly where, but
in the flood of 1785, so great a weight of water standing
over the grave, caused the earth to settle where it had
once been disturbed, and when the flood went down, a
sunken spot, exactly of the form and size of the grave, revealed its locality; but this was now lost again, and no future flood can detect it; yet, no doubt, Nature will know

now to point it out in due time, if it be necessary, by methods yet more searching and unexpected. Thus there is not only the crisis when the spirit ceases to inspire and expand the body, marked by a fresh mound in the churchyard, but there is also a crisis when the body ceases to take up room as such in nature, marked by a fainter depression in the earth.

"Friday," *A Week on the Concord and Merrimack Rivers,* 356–57

Arrowheads

It is remarkable that the spots where I find most arrowheads, etc., being light, dry soil, — as the Great Fields, Clamshell Hill, etc., — are among the first to be bare of snow, and the frost gets out there first. It is very curiously and particularly true, for the only parts of the northeast section of the Great Fields which are so dry that I do not slump there are those small in area, where perfectly bare patches of sand occur, and there, singularly enough, the arrowheads are particularly common. Indeed, in some cases I find them only on such bare spots a rod or two in extent where a single wigwam might have stood, and not half a dozen rods off in any direction. Yet the difference of level may not be more than a foot, — if there is any. It is as if the Indians had selected precisely the driest spots on the whole plain, with a view to their advantage at this season.

13 March 1859, *Journal* XII: 43–44

They are sown, like a grain that is slow to germinate, broadcast over the earth. Like the dragon's teeth which bore a crop of soldiers, these bear crops of philosophers and poets, and the same seed is just as good to plant again. It is a stone fruit. Each one yields me a thought I come nearer to the maker of it than if I found his bones. His bones would not prove any wit that wielded them, such as this work of his bones does. It is humanity inscribed on the face of the earth, patent to my eyes as soon as the snow goes off, not hidden away in some crypt or grave or under a pyramid. No disgusting mummy, but a clean stone, the best symbol or letter that could have been transmitted to me.

The Red Man, his mark

At every step I see it, and I can easily supply the "Tahatawan" or "Mantatuket" that might have been written if he had had a clerk. It is no single inscription on a particular rock, but a footprint — rather a mind-print — left everywhere, and altogether illegible. No vandals, however vandalic in their disposition, can be so industrious as to destroy them.

28 March 1859, *Journal* XII: 90–91

The Moose Hunt

Here, about two o'clock, we turned up a small branch three or four rods wide, which comes in on the right from the south, called Pine Stream, to look for moose signs. We had gone but a few rods before we saw very recent signs along the water's edge, the mud lifted up by their feet being quite fresh, and Joe declared that they had gone along there but a short time before. We soon reached a small meadow on the east side, at an angle in the stream, which was for the most part densely covered with alders. As we were advancing along the edge of this, rather more quietly than usual, perhaps, on account of the freshness of the signs, — the design being to camp up this stream, if it promised well, — I heard a slight crackling of twigs deep in the alders, and turned Joe's attention to it. Whereupon he began to push the canoe back rapidly, and we had receded thus half a dozen rods, when we suddenly spied two moose standing just on the edge of the open part of the meadow which we had passed, not more than six or seven rods distant, looking round the alders at us. They made me think of great frightened rabbits, with their long ears and half inquisitive half frightened looks; the true denizens of the forest, (I saw at once), filling a vacuum which now first I discovered had not been filled for me, — *Moose*-men, *woodeaters,* the word is said to mean — clad in a sort of Vermont gray or homespun. Our Nimrod, owing to the retrograde movement, was now the furthest from the game, but being warned of its neighborhood, he hastily stood up, and, while we ducked, fired over our heads, one barrel at the foremost, which alone he saw, though he did not know what kind of creature it was; whereupon this one dashed across the meadow and up a high bank on the north-east, so rapidly as to leave but an indistinct impression of its outlines on my mind. At the same instant, the other, a young one, but as tall as a horse, leaped out into the stream, in full sight, and there stood cowering for a moment, or rather its disproportionate lowness behind gave it that appearance, and uttering two or three trumpeting squeaks. I have an indistinct recollection of seeing the old one pause an instant on the top of the bank in the woods, look toward its shivering young, and then dash away again. The second barrel was levelled at the calf, and we expected to see it drop in the water, after a little hesitation, it too got out of the water and dashed up the hill, though in a somewhat different direction. All this was the work of a few seconds, and our hunter having never seen a moose before, did not know but they were deer, for they stood partly in the water, nor whether he had fired at the same one twice or not. From the style in which they went off, and the fact that he was not used to standing up and firing from a canoe, I judged that we should not see anything more of them. The Indian said that they were a cow and her calf—a yearling, or perhaps two years old, for they accompany their dams so long,—but for my part I had not noticed much difference in their size. It was but two or three rods across the meadow to the foot of the bank, which like all the world thereabouts was densely wooded, but I was surprised to notice, that as soon as the moose had passed behind the veil of the woods, there was no sound of footsteps to be heard from the soft damp moss which carpets that forest, and long before we landed perfect silence reigned. Joe said, "if you wound em moose, me sure get 'em."

We all landed at once. My companion reloaded; the Indian fastened his birch, threw off his hat—adjusted his waistband, seized the hatchet, and set out. He told me afterward, casually, that before we landed he had seen a drop of blood on the bank, when it was two or three rods off. He proceeded rapidly up the bank and through the woods, with a peculiar, elastic, noiseless, and stealthy tread, looking to right and left on the ground, and stepping in the faint tracks of the wounded moose, now and then pointing in silence to a single drop of blood on the handsome shining leaves of the *Clintonia borealis,* which on every side covered the ground, or to a dry fern stem freshly broken, all the while chewing some leaf or else the spruce gum. I followed, watching his motions more than the trail of the moose. After following the trail about forty rods in a pretty direct course, stepping over fallen trees and winding between standing ones, he at length lost it, for there were many other moose tracks there, and returning once more to the last blood stain traced it a little way and lost it again, and, too soon, I thought, for a good hunter, gave it up entirely. He traced a few steps also the tracks of the calf, but seeing no blood, soon relinquished the search.

I observed while he was tracking the moose a certain reticence or moderation in him. He did not communicate several observations of interest which he made, as a white man would have done, though they may have leaked out afterward. At another time, when we heard a slight crackling of twigs and he landed to reconnoitre, he stepped lightly and gracefully, stealing through the bushes with the least possible noise, in a way in which no white man does, as it were, finding a place for his foot each time.

About half an hour after seeing the moose, we pursued our voyage up Pine Stream, and soon, coming to a part which was very shoal and also rapid, we took out the baggage, and proceeded to carry it round, while Joe got up with the canoe alone. We were just completing our portage, and I was absorbed in the plants, admiring the leaves of the aster macrophyllus, ten inches wide, and plucking the seeds of the great round-leaved orchis, when Joe exclaimed from the stream that he had killed a moose. He had found the cow moose lying dead, but quite warm, in the middle of the stream, which was so shallow that it rested on the bottom, with hardly a third of its body above water. It was about an hour after it was shot, and it was swollen with water. It had run about a hundred rods and sought the stream again, cutting off a slight bend. No doubt a better hunter would have tracked it to this spot at once...

...The afternoon's tragedy, and my share in it, as it affected the innocence, destroyed the pleasure of my adventure. It is true, I came as near to being a hunter and miss it, as possible myself, and as it is, I think that I could spend a year in the woods, fishing and hunting just enough to sustain myself, with satisfaction. This would be next to living like a philosopher on the fruits of the earth which you had raised, which also attracts me. But this hunting of the moose merely for the satisfaction of killing him—not even for the sake of his hide, without making any extraordinary exertion or running any risk yourself, is too much like going out by night to some woodside pasture and shooting your neighbor's horses. These are God's own horses, poor timid creatures that will run fast enough as soon as they smell you, though they *are* nine feet high. Joe told us of some hunters who a year or two before had shot down several oxen by night, somewhere in the Maine woods, mistaking them for moose. And so might any of the hunters; and what is the difference in the sport, but the name? In the former case, having killed one of God's and *your own* oxen, you strip off its hide, because that is the common trophy, and moreover you have heard that it may be sold for moccasins, cut a steak from its haunches, and leave the huge carcass to smell to heaven for you. It is no better, at least, than to assist at a slaughter house.

"Chesuncook," *The Maine Woods,* 109–19

Savage Meets Savage

When a new country like North America is discovered, a few feeble efforts are made to Christianize the natives before they are all exterminated, but they are not found to pay, in any sense. But the energetic traders of the discovering country organize themselves, or rather inevitably crystallize, into a vast rat-catching society, tempt the natives to become mere vermin-hunters and rum-drinkers, reserving half a continent for the field of their labors. Savage meets savage, and the white man's only distinction is that he is the chief.

8 April 1859, *Journal* XII: 124

The Historian and the Indian

Some have spoken slightingly of the Indians, as a race possessing so little skill and wit, so low in the scale of humanity, and so brutish that they hardly deserved to be remembered, — using only the terms "miserable," "wretched," "pitiful," and the like. In writing their histories of this country they have so hastily disposed of this refuse of humanity (as they might have called it) which littered and defiles the shore and the interior. But even the indigenous animals are inexhaustibly interesting to us. How much more, then, the indigenous man of America! If wild men, so much more like ourselves than they are unlike, have inhabited these shores before us, we wish to know particularly what manner of men they were, how they lived here, their relation to nature, their arts and their customs, their fancies and superstitions. They paddled over these waters, they wandered in these woods, and they had their fancies and beliefs connected with the sea and the forest, which concern us quite as much as the fables of Oriental nations do. It frequently happens that the historian, though he professes more humanity than the trapper, mountain man, or gold-digger, who shoots one as a wild beast, really exhibits and practices a similar inhumanity to him, wielding a pen instead of a rifle.

3 February 1859, *Journal* XI: 437–38

Plowing Up the Land

For the Indian there is no safety but in the plow. If he would not be pushed into the Pacific, he must seize hold of a plow-tail and let go his bow and arrow, his fish-spear and rifle. This the only Christianity that will save him.

His fate says sternly to him, "Forsake the hunter's life and enter into the agricultural, the second, state of man. Root yourselves a little deeper in the soil, if you would continue to be the occupants of the country."

But I confess I have no little sympathy with the Indians and hunter men. They seem to be a distinct and equally respectable people, born to wander and to hunt, and not to be inoculated with the twilight civilization of the white man.

Father Le Jeuune, a French missionary, affirmed "that the Indians were superior in intellect to the French peasantry of that time," and advised "that laborers should be sent from France in order to work for the Indians."

The Indian population within the present boundaries of New Hampshire, Massachusetts, Rhode Island, and

Connecticut has been estimated not to have exceeded 40,000 "before the epidemic disease which preceded the landing of the Pilgrims," and it was far more dense here than elsewhere; yet they had no more land than they wanted. The present white population is more than 1,500,000 and two thirds of the land is unimproved.

The Indian, perchance, has not made up his mind to some things which the white man has consented to; he has not, in all respects, stooped so low; and hence, though he too loves food and warmth, he draws his tattered blanket about him and follows his fathers, rather than barter his birthright. He dies, and no doubt his Genius judges well for him. But he is not worsted in the fight; he is not destroyed. He only migrates beyond the Pacific to more spacious and happier hunting-grounds.

A race of hunters can never withstand the inroads of a race of husbandmen. The latter burrow in the night into their country and undermine them; and [even] if the hunter is brave enough to resist, his game is timid and has already fled. The rifle alone would never exterminate it, but the plow is a more fatal weapon; it wins the country inch by inch and holds all it gets.

What detained the Cherokees so long was the 2923 plows which that people possessed; and if they had grasped their handles more firmly, they would never have been driven beyond the Mississippi. No sense of justice will ever restrain the farmer from plowing up the land which is only hunted over by his neighbors. No hunting-field was ever well fenced and surveyed and its bounds accurately marked, unless it were an English park. It is a property not held by the hunter so much as by the game which roams it, and was never well secured by warranty deeds. The farmer in his treaties says only, or means only, "So far will I plow this summer," for he has not seed corn enough to plant more; but every summer the seed is grown which plants a new strip of the forest.

1837–1847, *Journal* I: 444–46

From Treetop to Quaking Swamp: A Rich, Diverse Land Mosaic

In "October Farm," William Brewster remarked how some birds have favourite singing-perches. Concord with its low hills, slow-pulsed winding river, wildwood openings and fields like thresholds was Thoreau's singing-perch. Planted casually in its lean soil, he germinated, took tenacious root in its pleasant rural landscape, matured, bore fruit, was early stricken and died, unvanquished in spirit, mingling the earth of him with the earth of Concord to which he was native. The spirit of his temperament was as native to its habitat as the river mists that hover perennially over the Muske-taquid. It was as indigenous as the smoke that rises from the freshly turned furrow of a strip of bottom land in Concord meadows. He loved Concord earth; his roots gripped its soil and he carried, as he said, figuratively, Concord ground in his boots and in his hat.

— Reginald Lansing Cook

Concord's Great Wild Tracts

What shall this great wild tract over which we strolled be called? Many farmers have pastures there, and wood-lots, and orchards. It consists mainly of rocky pastures. It contains what I call the Boulder Field, the Yellow Birch Swamp, the Black Birch Hill, the Laurel Pasture, the Hog-Pasture, the White Pine Grove, the Easterbrooks

Place, the Old Lime-Kiln, the Lime Quarries, Spruce Swamp, the Ermine Weasel Woods; also the Oak Meadows, the Cedar Swamp, the Kibbe Place, and the old place northwest of Brooks Clark's. Ponkawtasset bounds it to the south. There are a few frog-ponds and an old mill-pond within it, and Bateman's Pond on its edge. What shall the whole be called? The old Carlisle road, which runs through the middle of it, is bordered on each side with wild apple pastures, where the trees stand without order, having, many if not most of them, sprung up by accident or from pomace sown at random, and are for the most part concealed by birches and pines. These orchards are very extensive, and yet many of these apple trees, growing as forest trees, bear good crops of apples. It is a paradise for walkers in the fall. There are also boundless huckleberry pastures as well as many blueberry swamps. Shall we call it the Easterbrooks Country? It would make a princely estate in Europe, yet it is owned by farmers, who live by the labor of their hands and do not esteem it much. Plenty of huckleberries and barberries here.

A second great uninhabited tract is that on the Marlborough road, stretching westerly from Francis Wheeler's to the river, and beyond about three miles, and from Harrington's on the north to Dakin's on the south, more than a mile in width. A third, the Walden Woods. A fourth, the Great Fields. These four are all in Concord.

10 June 1853, *Journal* V: 239-40

I Walk Toward Oregon

It is hard for me to believe that I shall find fair landscapes or sufficient wildness and freedom behind the eastern horizon. I am not excited by the prospect of a walk thither; but I believe that the forest which I see in the western horizon stretches uninterruptedly toward the setting sun, and there are no towns nor cities in it of enough consequence to disturb me. Let me live where I will, on this side is the city, on that the wilderness, and ever I am leaving the city more and more, and withdrawing into the wilderness. I should not lay so much stress on this fact, if I did not believe that something like this is the prevailing tendency of my countrymen. I must walk toward Oregon, and not toward Europe.

"Walking," 105–6

Our River

I think our overflowing river — far handsomer & more abounding in soft and beautiful contrasts — than a merely broad river would be — A succession of bays it is — a chain of lakes — an endlessly scolloped shore — — rounding wood & field — cultivated field & wood & pasture and house are brought into ever new & unexpected positions & relations to the water. There is just stream enough for a flow of thought — that is all.

16 April 1852, *Journal* 4: 458

A Distant Valley

Far away from here, in Lancaster, with another companion, I have crossed the broad valley of the Nashua, over which we had so long looked westward from the Concord hills without seeing it to the blue mountains in the horizon. So many streams, so many meadows and woods and quiet dwellings of men had lain concealed between us and those Delectable Mountains; — from yonder hill on the road to Tyngsboro' you may get a good view of them. — There where it seemed uninterrupted forest to our youthful eyes, between two neighboring pines in the horizon, lay the valley of the Nashua, and this very stream was even then winding at its bottom, and then, as now, it was here silently mingling its waters with the Merrimack. The clouds which floated over its meadows and were born there, seen far in the west, gilded by the rays of the setting sun, had adorned a thousand evening skies for us. But as it were, by a turf wall this valley was concealed, and in our journey to those hills it was first gradually revealed to us. Summer and winter our eyes had rested on the dim outline of the mountains, to which distance and indistinctness lent a grandeur not their own, so that they served to interpret all the allusions of poets and travellers. Standing on the Concord Cliffs we thus spoke our mind to them.

"Monday," *A Week on the Concord and Merrimack Rivers*, 162–63

Stone Walls

I sometimes see well preserved walls running straight through the midst of high & old woods — built of course when the soil was cultivated many years ago — and am surprised to see slight stones still lying one upon another as the builder placed them while this huge oak has grown up from a chance acorn on the soil.

9 November 1850, *Journal* 3: 136

A Million Concords

I too love Concord best — But I am glad when I discover in oceans & wildernesses far away the materials out of which a million Concords can be made. Indeed unless I discover them I am lost myself. That there too I am at home.

After 29 July 1850, Journal 3: 97

The Geologist

The most inattentive walker can see how the science of geology took its rise. The inland hills & promontories betray the action of water on their rounded sides as plainly as if the work were completed yesterday. He sees it with but half an eye as he walks & forgets his thought again. Also the level plains & more recent meadows & marine shells found on the tops of hills — The Geologist painfully & elaborately follows out these suggestions — & hence his fine spun theories.

19 August 1851, Journal 3: 379

A Star Dropped Down

We hug the earth, — how rarely we mount! Methinks we might elevate ourselves a little more. We might climb a tree, at least. I found my account in climbing a tree once. It was a tall white pine, on the top of a hill; and though I got well pitched, I was well paid for it, for I discovered new mountains in the horizon which I had never seen before, — so much more of the earth and heavens. I might have walked about the foot of the tree for threescore years and ten, and yet I certainly should never have seen them. But, above all, I discovered around me, — it was near the end of June, — on the ends of the topmost branches only, a few minute and delicate red cone-like blossoms, the fertile flower of the white pine looking heavenward. I carried straightaway to the village the topmost spire, and showed it to stranger jurymen who walked the streets, —

for it was court-week, — and to farmers and lumber-dealers and wood-choppers and hunters, and not one had ever seen the like before, but they wondered as at a star dropped down.

"Walking," 132–33

I Keep a Mountain

I keep a mountain anchored off eastward a little way, which I ascend in my dreams both awake and asleep. Its broad base spreads over a village or two, which do not know it; neither does it know them, nor do I when I ascend it. I can see its general outline as plainly now in my mind as that of Wachusett. I do not invent in the least, but state exactly what I see. I find that I go up it when I am light-footed and earnest. It ever smokes like an altar with its sacrifice. I am not aware that a single villager frequents it or knows of it. I keep this mountain to ride instead of a horse.

16 November 1857, Letter to H. G. O. Blake,
Correspondence, 498

A Small Brook

Sat awhile before sun-set on the rocks in Saw Mill Brook — A brook need not be large to afford us pleasure by its sands & meanderings and falls & their various accompaniments. It is not so much size that we want as picturesque beauty & harmony.

1 April 1852, Journal 4: 412

No Particular Landscape

There is some advantage perhaps in attending to the general features of the landscape over studying the particular plants & animals which inhabit it. A man may walk abroad & no more see the sky than if he walked under a shed. The poet is more in the air than the naturalist though they may walk side by side. — Granted that you are out of door — but what if the outer door *is* open, if the inner door is shut. You must walk sometimes perfectly free — not prying nor inquisitive — not bent upon seeing things — Throw away a whole day for a single expansion. a single inspiration of air —

21 August 1851, *Journal* 4: 6

Writing by Moonlight

Moon not quite full. Going across Depot Field. The western sky is now a crescent of saffron inclining to salmon, a little dunnish, perhaps. The grass is wet with dew. The evening star has come out, but no other. There is no wind. I see a nighthawk in the twilight, flitting near the ground. I hear the hum of a beetle going by. The greenish fires of lightning-bugs are already seen in the meadow. I almost lay my hand on one amid the leaves as I get over the fence at the brook. I pass through Hubbardston along the side of a field of oats, which wet one leg. I perceive the smell of a burning far off by the river, which I saw smoking two days ago. The moon is laboring in a mackerel cloud, and my hopes are with her. Why do I hear no bullfrogs yet? Do they ever trump as early and as universally as on that first evening? I hear the whip-poor-wills on different sides. White flowers alone show much at night, — white clover and whiteweed. It is commonly still at night, as now. The day has gone by with its wind like the wind of a cannon-ball, and now far in the west it blows. By that dun-colored sky you may track it. There is

Tamed savage

no motion nor sound in the woods (Hubbard's Grove) along which I am walking. The trees stand like great screens against the sky. The distant village sounds are the barking of dogs, that animal with which man has allied himself, and the rattling of wagons, for the farmers have gone into town a-shopping this Saturday night. The dog is the tamed wolf, as the villager is the tamed savage. But near, the crickets are heard in the grass, chirping from everlasting to everlasting, a mosquito sings near my ear, and the humming of a dor-bug drowns all the noise of the village, so roomy is the universe. The moon comes out of the mackerel cloud, and the traveller rejoices. How can a man write the same thoughts by the light of the moon, resting his book on a rail by the side of a remote potato-field, that he does by the light of the sun, on his study table? The light is but a luminousness. My pencil seems to move through a creamy, mystic medium. The moon-light is rich and somewhat opaque, like cream, but the daylight is thin and blue, like skimmed milk. I am less conscious than in the presence of the sun; my instincts have more influence. I love the smell of that burning as a man may his pipe. It reminds me of a new country offering sites for the hearths of men. It is cheering as the scent of the peat fire of the first settler. The farmer has improved the dry weather to burn his meadow.

18 June 1853, *Journal* V: 277–78

Pleasant Variations

What can be handsomer for a picture than our river scenery now! Take this view from the first Conantum Cliff. First this smoothly shorne meadow on the west side of the stream, with all the swathes distinct — Sprinkled with apple trees casting heavy shadows — black as ink, such as can be seen only in this clear air. — this strong light — one cow wandering restlessly about in it and lowing. — Then the blue river — scarcely darker than and not to be distinguished from the sky — its waves driven sowthward or up stream by the wind — making it appear to flow that way bordered by willows & button bushes. — Then the narrow meadow beyond with varied lights & shades from its waving grass which for some reason has not been cut this year. — though so dry — now at length each grass blade bending south before the wintery blast, as if bending for aid in that direction. — Then the hill rising 60 feet to a terrace like plain — covered with shruboaks — maples &c now variously tinted. clad all in a livery of gay colors — every bush a feather in its cap. And further in the rear the wood crowned Cliff some 200 feet high, where grey rocks here & there project from amidst the bushes. — with its orchard on the slope. And to the right of the cliff the distant Lincoln hills in the horizon. The landscape so handsomely colored — the air so clear & wholesome — & the surface of the earth is so pleasingly varied — that it seems rarely fitted for the abode of man.

24 September 1851, *Journal* 4: 94

A Broad Country

Our Country is broad and rich — for here within 20 miles of Boston I can stand in a clearing in the woods and look a mile or more over the shrub oaks to the distant pine copses and horizon of uncut woods without a house or road or cultivated field in sight.

20 December 1851, *Journal* 4: 212

View from a Hill

The prospect is often best from ²/₃ the way up a hill —
where looking directly down at the parts of the landscape
— the fields & barns — nearest the base, you get the sense
of height best — & see how the land slopes up to where
you stand — From the top commonly you over look all
this — and merely get a sense of *distance* merely — with a
break in the landscape by which the most interesting part
is concealed.

2 April 1852, *Journal* 4: 421

Boulders in a Storm

In the pasture beyond the brook where grow the barberries — huckleberries — creeping juniper &c are half a
dozen huge boulders which look grandly now in the
storm covered with greenish gray lichens alternating with
the slateish colored rock. Slumbering — silent like the ex-
uviae of Giants — some of their cattle left. From a height I
look down on some of them as on the backs of oxen. A
certain personality or at least brute life they seem to have.

21 April 1852, *Journal* 4: 480

Like Islands in the Fog

Looking now from the rocks — the fog is a perfect sea
over the great Sudbury meadows in the S W — commencing at the base of this cliff & reaching to the hills
south of Wayland & further still to Framingham —
through which only the tops of the higher hills are seen
as islands — great bays of the sea many miles across
where the largest fleets would find ample room — & in
which countless farms & farm houses are immersed. The
fog rises highest over the channel of the river and over the

ponds in the woods which are thus revealed—I clearly distinguish where white pond lies by this sign—and various other ponds methinks to which I have walked 10 or 12 miles distant, & I distinguish the course of the assabet far in the west & SW beyond the woods Every valley is densely packed with the downy vapor— What levelling on a great scale is done thus for the eye!

25 July 1852, *Journal* 5: 247

Patches of Rye

The patches of winter rye, at this season so green by contrast are an interesting feature in the landscape—When I got out of the wood, going toward Barretts—the softness of the sun-light on the russet landscape—the smooth russet grassy fields & meadows, was very soothing—the sun now getting low in a november day.

29 November 1852, *Journal* 5: 399–400

Crooked Walls

Excepting those fences which are mere boundaries of individual property—the walker can generally perceive the reason for those which he is obliged to get over— This wall runs along just on the edge of the hill & following all its windings to separate the more level & cultivateable summit from the slope which is only fit for pasture—or woodlot—& that other wall below divides the pasture or woodlot—from the richer low grass ground or potatoe field. &c- Even these crooked walls are not always unaccountable & lawless.

12 July 1852, *Journal* 5: 219

Absorbed in Details

At this season methinks we do not regard the larger features of the landscape—as in the spring—but are absorbed in details— Thus when the meadows were flooded I looked far over them—to the distant woods & the outlines of hills which were more distinct. I should not have so much to say of extensive water or landscapes at this season— You are a little bewildered by the variety of objects. There must be a certain meagreness of details and nakedness for wide views.

2 July 1852, *Journal* 5: 174

Meadow & Stream

There is a meadow on the Assabet just above Derby's Bridge—it may contain an acre bounded on one side by the river on the other by alders and a hill—completely covered with small hummocks which have loged on it in the winter—covering it like the mounds in a graveyard at pretty regular intervals— Their edges are rounded like latter and they and the paths between are covered with a firm short green sward—with here and there hard hacks springing out of them—so that they make excellent seats—especially in the shade of an elm that grows there— They are completely united with the meadow—forming little oblong hillocks from 1 to 10 feet long—flat as a mole to the sward— I am inclined to call it the elphin burial ground. It is a remarkably firm swarded meadow & convenient to walk on. And these hummock have an important effect in elevating it. It suggests at once a burial ground of the aborigines—where perchance lie the earthly remains of the rude forefathers of the race. I love to ponder the natural history thus written

on the banks of the stream— for every higher freshet &
intenser frost is recorded by it— The stream keeps a
faithful & a true journal of every event in its experience
—whatever race may settle on its banks and it purls past
this natural grave-yard with a storied murmur—& no
doubt it could find endless employment for an old mor-
tality in renewing its epitaphs.

5 July 1852, *Journal* 5: 184–85

What a Wonder a River Is

For the first time it occurred to me this afternoon what a
piece of wonder a river is.— A huge volume of matter
ceaselessly rolling through the fields and meadows of this
substantial earth—making haste from the high places, by
stable dwellings of men and Egyptian pyramids; to its
restless reservoir— One would think that, by a very natural impulse, the dwellers upon the headwaters of the
Mississippi and Amazon, would follow in the trail of
their waters to see the end of the matter.

5 September 1838, *Journal* 1: 55

Nature Breathes over All

East west north and south it is hill and valley forest and
plain this earth of ours—one may see how at convenient
intervals men have settled themselves—without thought
for the universe—But How little matters it all men have
built and delved there in the valley, it is but a feature in
the landscape. Still the vast impulse of nature breathes
over all;—the eternal winds sweep across the interval today, bringing mist and haze to shut out their works. Still
the crow caws from hill to hill—as no feeble tradesman

nor smith may do — and in all swamps the hum of mosquitoes drowns this modern hum of industry.

Transcribed 1842, *Journal* 1: 406–7

Puny Fences

I am amused to see from my window here how busily
man has divided and staked off his domain. God must
smile at his puny fences running hither and thither everywhere over the land.

20 February 1842, *Journal* 1: 365

Through a Looking Glass

I am brought into the near neighborhood — and am become a silent observer of the moon's paces to-night by
means of a glass — while the frogs are peeping all around
me on the earth — and the sound of the accordion seems
to come from some bright saloon yonder. I am sure the
moon floats in a human atmosphere — it is but a distant
scene of the world's drama. It is a wide theater the gods
have given us, and our actions must befit it

2 June 1841, *Journal* 1: 312

The Lake

The lake is a mirror in the breast of nature, as if there
were nothing to be concealed. All the sins of the wood
are washed out in it. See how the woods form an am-
phitheatre about it — and becomes an arena for all the ge-
nialness of nature. It is the earth's liquid eye — it is blue
or grey, or black as I choose my time. In the night it is my
more than forty feet reflector. It is the cynosure of the
wood, all trees direct the traveller to its brink — all paths
seek it out — birds fly to it — and quadrupeds flee to it —

and the very ground inclines toward it. It is nature's saloon, or where she has sat down to her toilet. The sun dusts its surface each morning by evaporation. Always a fresh surface wells up. I love to consider the silent economy and tidiness of nature, how after all the filth of the wood, and the accumulated impurities of the winter have been rinsed herein, this liquid transparency appears in the spring.

2 December 1840, *Journal* 1: 198–99

Standing in a Swamp

Would it not be a luxury to stand up to ones chin in some retired swamp for a whole summer's day, scenting the sweet fern and bilberry blows, and lulled by the minstrelsy of gnats and mosquitoes? A day passed in the society of those Greek sages, such as described in the "Banquet" of Xenophon, would not be comparable with the dry wit of decayed cranberry vines, and the fresh Attic salt of the moss beds. Say twelve hours of genial and familiar converse with the leopard frog. The sun to rise behind alder and dogwood, and climb boyantly to his meridian of three hands' breadth — and finally sink to rest behind some bold western hummock. To hear the evening chant of the mosquito from a thousand green chapels — and the bittern begin to boom from his concealed fort — like a sunset gun!

16 July 1840, *Journal* 1: 129

An Admirable Fence

In the sunrise I see an eastern city with its spires, in the sunset a western forest. — The woods are an admirable fence to the landscape — every where skirting the horizon.

Walk Toward Rutland

I remember that walk to Asnebumskit very well; — a fit place to go on a Sunday, one of the true temples of the earth. A temple you know was anciently "an open place without a roof," whose walls served merely to shut out the world, and direct the mind toward heaven; but a modern *meeting house* shuts out the heavens, while it crowds the world into still closer quarters. Best of all is it when as on a *Mt.* top you have for all walls your own elevations and deeps of surrounding ether. The partridge berries watered with *Mt.* dews, which are gathered there, are more memorable to me than the words which I last heard from the pulpit at least, and for my part I would rather walk toward Rutland than Jerusalem. Rutland — modern town — land of ruts — trivial and worn — not too sacred — with no holy sepulchre, but prophane green fields and dusty roads, — and opportunity to live as holy life as you can; — where the sacredness if there is any is all in yourself and not in the place.

All Earth a Garden

We are wont to forget that the sun looks on our cultivated fields and on the prairies and forests without distinction. They all reflect and absorb his rays alike, and the former make but a small part of the glorious picture which he beholds in his daily course. In his view the earth is all equally cultivated like a garden. Therefore we should receive the benefit of his light and heat with a corresponding trust and magnanimity.

"The Bean-Field," Walden, 166

Reverence for the Earth

When the common man looks into the sky, which he has not so much profaned, he thinks it less gross than the earth, and with reverence speaks of "the Heavens," but the seer will in the same sense speak of "the Earths," and his Father who is in them.

"Friday," A Week on the Concord
and Merrimack Rivers, 382

A Nobler Road Through the Landscape

Flag Hill is about 8 miles by the road from Concord — we went much further going & returning both. But by how much nobler road — Suppose you were to ride to Boxboro what then? — You pass a few teams with their dust — drive through many farmers' barnyards — between two walls — see where Squire Tuttle lives & barrels his apples. Bait your horse at White's tavern & so return with your hands smelling of greasy leather & horse-hair — & the squeak of a chaise body in your ears — with no new flower nor agreeable experience — But going as we did before you got to Boxboro line — you often went much further — many times ascended N.H. hills — Taking the noble road from hill to hill across swamps and vallies — not regarding political courses & boundaries — many times far west in your thought — It is a journey of a day & a picture of human life.

19 June 1852, Journal 5: 117

Pleasure from the Landscape

A healthy and refined nature would always derive pleasure from the landscape.

27 June 1852, *Journal* 5: 157

The World Can Never Be More Beautiful

The world can never be more beautiful than now—for combined with the tender fresh green you have this remarkable clearness of the air. I doubt if the landscape will be any greener. The landscape is most beautiful looking towards the sun (in the orchard on Fair Haven) at 4+. 1st there is this green slope on which I sit looking down between the rows of apple trees just being clothed with tender green.—sometimes under neath them to the sparkling water—or over through them—or seeing them against the sky. 2ndly the outline of this bank or hill is drawn against the waters far below—the river still high—a beautifully bright sheen on the water there—though it is elsewhere a dull slaty blue color—a sober rippled surface.— A fine sparkling shimmer in front—owing to the remarkable clearness of the atmosphere (Clarified by the May storm?)

Thirdly on either side of the wood beyond the river—are patches of bright tender yellowish velvety green grass in meadows & on hill-sides. It is like a short furred mantle now—& bright as if it had the sun on it.— These great fields of green affect me as did those early green blades by the Corner spring—like a fire flaming up from the earth. The earth proves itself well alive even in the skin. No scurf on it only a browner color on the barren tops of hills. 4thly the forest the dark green pines wonderfully distinct—near—& erect—with their distinct dark stems spiring tops — regularly disposed branches, & silvery light on their needles. They seem to wear an aspect as much fresher & livelier as the other trees — though their growth can hardly be perceptible yet — as if they had been washed by the rains & the air — They are now being invested with the light sunny yellowish green of the deciduous trees — This tender foliage — putting so much light & life into the landscape is the remarkable feature at this date. The week when the deciduous trees are generally and conspicuously expanding their leaves. The various tints of grey oaks — & yellowish green birches & aspens & hickories — & the red or scarlet tops where maple keys are formed — (the blossoms are now over) these last the high color (rosaceous?) in the bouquet. — And 5thly I detect a great stretch of high backed mostly bare grassy pasture country between this & the Nashua — spotted with pines & forests. — which I had formerly taken for forest uninterrupted. & finally 6thly Wachusett rising in the background slightly veiled in bluish mist, — toward which all these seem to slope gradually upward — and those grassy hill sides in the foreground — seen but as patches of bare grassy ground on a spur of that distant *Mt.*

18 May 1852, *Journal* 5: 65–67

Like Leaves of the Choicest Volume

The delicacy of the stratification in the white sand by the RR — where they have been getting out sand for the brickyards — the delicate stratification of this great globe like the leaves of the choicest volume just shut on a ladies table — The piled up history! I am struck by the slow & delicate process by which the globe was formed.

12 October 1852, *Journal* 5: 370

A Loud Cracking of the Ground

Walked a little way along the bank of the Merrimack, which was frozen over, and was agreeably reminded of my voyage up it. The night previous, in Amherst, I had been awaked by the loud cracking of the ground, which shook the house like the explosion of a powder-mill. In the morning there was to be seen a long crack across the road in front. I saw several of these here in Nashua, and ran a bit of stubble into them but in no place more than five inches. This is a sound peculiar to the coldest nights. Observed that the Nashua in Pepperell was frozen to the very edge of the fall, and even further in some places.

18 December 1856, *Journal* IX: 189

Wildness and the Human Spirit

"Walking" is one of Thoreau's better-known essays today because its advocacy of the wild is the philosophical cornerstone of twentieth-century movements to preserve wilderness tracts in America. Yet Thoreau did not think of the wild — or of walking either — as a special preserve. It was not for recreation so much as it was for re-creation; it was a particular quality of life that had to be actively cultivated. The spirit of the walk and not the specific route makes one a true saunterer.... Similarly, the wild has less to do with actual wilderness areas... than it does with a habit of mind which recognizes the balance of mutually dependent forces in life.... The wild is a reminder of an original attachment to the sources of life, and points back to a time and a state where nature and man's consciousness were not separate entities, and where nature was not an object to be learned and mastered for the sake of material knowledge and power.

— Robert Sattelmeyer

Out of My Senses

I feel a little alarmed when it happens that I have walked a mile into the woods bodily, without getting there in spirit. I would fain forget all my morning's occupation — my obligations to society. But sometimes it happens that

I cannot easily shake off the village — the thought of some work — some surveying will run in my head and I am not where my body is — I am out of my senses. In my walks I would return to my senses like a bird or a beast. What business have I in the woods if I am thinking of something out of the woods.

25 November 1850, Journal 3: 150

Free from Worldly Engagements

I think that I cannot preserve my health and spirits, unless I spend four hours a day at least, — and it is commonly more than that, — sauntering through the woods over the hills and fields, absolutely free from all worldly engagements. You may safely say, A penny for your thoughts, or a thousand pounds. When sometimes I am reminded that the mechanics and shopkeepers stay in their shops not only all the forenoon, but all the afternoon too, sitting with crossed legs, many of them, — as if the legs were made to sit upon, and not to stand or walk upon, — I think that they deserve some credit for not having all committed suicide long ago.

"Walking," 95–96

The Tonic for Mankind

The West of which I speak is but another name for the Wild; and what I have been preparing to say is, that in Wildness is the preservation of the World. Every tree sends its fibres forth in search of the Wild. The cities import it at any price. Men plough and sail for it. From the forest and wilderness come the tonics and barks which brace mankind.

"Walking," 112

Give Me Wild Men

In short, all good things are wild and free. There is something in a strain of music, whether produced by an instrument or by the human voice, — take the sound of a bugle in a summer night, for instance, — which by its wildness, to speak without satire, reminds me of the cries emitted by wild beasts in their native forests. It is so much of their wildness as I can understand. Give me for my friends and neighbors wild men, not tame ones. The wildness of the savage is but a faint symbol of the awful ferity with which good men and lovers meet.

"Walking," 122

Seeds of Instinct

I love even to see the domestic animals reassert their native rights, — any evidence that they have not wholly lost their original wild habits and vigor; as when my neighbor's cow breaks out of her pasture early in the spring and boldly swims the river, a cold, gray tide, twenty-five or thirty rods wide, swollen by the melted snow. It is the buffalo crossing the Mississippi. This exploit confers some dignity on the herd in my eyes, — already dignified. The seeds of instinct are preserved under the thick hides of cattle and horses, like seeds in the bowels of the earth, an indefinite period.

"Walking," 122

This Savage Howling Mother

Here is this vast, savage howling mother of ours, Nature, lying all around, with such beauty, and such affection for her children, as the leopard; and yet we are so early weaned from her breast to society, to that culture which is exclusively an interaction of man on man, — a sort of

breeding in and in, which produces at most a merely
English nobility, a civilization destined to have a speedy
limit.

"Walking," 125

An Attraction to Nature

While almost all men feel an attraction drawing them to
society, few are attracted strongly to Nature. In their relation to Nature men appear to me for the most part,
notwithstanding their arts, lower than the animals. It is
not often a beautiful relation, as in the case of the animals.
How little appreciation of the beauty of the landscape
there is among us! We have to be told that the Greeks
called the world Beauty, or Order, but we do not see
clearly why they did so, and we esteem it at best only a
curious philological fact.

"Walking," 129–30

A Cockerel Crow

When in doleful slumps, breaking the awful stillness of
our wooden sidewalk on a Sunday, or, perchance, a
watcher in the house of mourning, I hear a cockerel crow
far or near, I think to myself "There is one of us well, at
any rate,"—and with a sudden gush return to my senses.

"Walking," 134

I Reverence Them Both

I found in myself, and still find, an instinct toward a
higher, or, as it is named, spiritual life, as do most men,
and another toward a primitive rank and savage one, and
I reverence them both.

"Higher Laws," *Walden,* 210

A Living Earth

The earth I tread on is not a dead inert mass. It is a body — has a spirit — is organic — and fluid to the influence of its spirit — and to whatever particle of that spirit is in me.

31 December 1851, *Journal* 4: 230

Owls

I rejoice that there are owls. They represent the stark twilight unsatisfied thoughts I have. Let owls do the idiotic & maniacal hooting for men.

18 November 1851, *Journal* 4: 192

Mountains Worthy of Worship

I go to Flints P. for the sake of the *Mt* view from the hill beyond looking over Concord. I have thought it the best especially in the winter which I can get in this neighborhood. It is worth the while to see the *Mts* in the horizon once a day. I have thus seen some earth which corresponds to my least earthly & trivial — to my most heavenward looking thoughts — The earth seen through an azure an etherial veil. They are the natural *temples* elevated brows of the earth — looking at which the thoughts of the beholder are naturally elevated and etherialized. I wish to see the earth through the medium of much air or heaven — for there is no paint like the air. *Mts* thus seen are worthy of worship.

12 September 1851, *Journal* 4: 75

Food for the Senses

A man should feed his senses with the best that the land affords

12 September 1851, *Journal* 4: 75

Ah Dear Nature

Ah dear nature—the mere remembrance, after a short forgetfulness, of the pine woods! I come to it as a hungry man to a crust of bread.

I have been surveying for 20 or 30 days—living coarsely—even as respects my diet—for I find that that will always alter to suit my employment— Indeed leading a quite trivial life—& tonight for the first time had made a fire in my chamber & endeavored to return to myself. I wished to ally myself to the powers that rule the universe— I wished to dive into some deep stream of thoughtful & devoted life—which meandered through retired & fertile meadows far from towns. I wished to do again—or for once, things quite congenial to my highest inmost and most sacred nature— To lurk in crystalline thought like the trout under verdurous banks—where stray mankind should only see my bubble come to the surface.

12 December 1851, *Journal* 4: 201

A Different Mill

It is a good school the farmer's sons go to these afternoons loading & hauling great mill logs bigger than any cannons—a sort of battle in the forest. I think there must be an excitement derived from their labor such as they cannot tell. After reading of the life & battles of the northmen in Snorro Sturleson's Chronicle—these labors most remind me of that. Some of these logs are for pumps — Most are for boards & timbers & spiles for bridges. I met one old pupil of mine stretched at his length upon a vast balista or battering ram of a log—while one yoke & loaded sled went on alone before & another followed behind. How they renew and wear out the paths through the woods! They think I'm loafing. I think they are drudging for gain. But no doubt our employment is more alike than we suspect — and we are each serving the great Master's ends more than our own — I have my work in the woods where I meet them, though my logs do not go to the same mill. I make a different use of skids

15 January 1852, *Journal* 4: 256–57

I Am a New Englander

— Dear to me to lie in — this sand — which will preserve the bones of a race for thousands of years. to come. And this is my home — my native soil, and I am a New Englander. Of thee o earth are my bone & sinew made — to thee o sun am I brother. It must be the largest lake in Middlesex. To this dust my body will gladly return as to its origin. Here have I my habitat. I am of thee. —

7 November 1851, *Journal* 4: 167

Wild Yet Refined

The works of man are every where swallowed up in the immensity of Nature. The Ægean Sea is but Lake Huron still to the Indian. Also there is all the refinement of civilized life in the woods under a sylvan garb. The wildest scenes have an air of domesticity and homeliness even to the citizen, and when the flicker's cackle is heard in the clearing, he is reminded that civilization has wrought but little change there. Science is welcome to the deepest recesses of the forest, for there too nature obeys the same old civil laws. The little red bug on the stump of a pine, for it the wind shifts and the sun breaks through the clouds. In the wildest nature, there is not only the material of the most cultivated life, and a sort of anticipation of the last result, but a greater refinement already than is ever attained by man.

"Thursday," *A Week on the Concord and Merrimack Rivers*, 316

The Winds Should Be His Breath

Men nowhere, east or west, live yet a *natural* life, round which the vine clings, and which the elm willingly shadows. Man would desecrate it by his touch, and so the beauty of the world remains veiled to him. He needs not only to be spiritualized, but *naturalized,* on the soil of the earth. Who shall conceive what kind of roof the heavens might extend over him, what seasons minister to him, and what employment dignify his life! Only the convalescent raise the veil of nature. An immortality in his life would confer immortality on his abode. The winds should be his breath, the seasons his moods, and he should impart of his serenity to Nature herself. But such as we know him he is ephemeral like the scenery which surrounds him, and does not aspire to an enduring existence. When we come down into the distant village, visible from the mountain top, the nobler inhabitants with whom we peopled it have departed, and left only vermin in its desolate streets. It is the imagination of poets which puts those brave speeches into the mouths of their heroes.

"Friday," *A Week on the Concord and Merrimack Rivers*, 379

Where the Pine Flourishes

The wilderness is near, as well as dear, to every man. Even the oldest villages are indebted to the border of wild wood which surrounds them, more than to the gar-

dens of men. There is something indescribably inspiriting and beautiful in the aspect of the forest skirting and
occasionally jutting into the midst of new towns, which,
like the sand-heaps of fresh fox burrows, have sprung up
in their midst. The very uprightness of the pines and
maples asserts the ancient rectitude and vigor of nature.
Our lives need the relief of such a back-ground, where
the pine flourishes and the jay still screams.

"Monday," *A Week on the Concord*
and Merrimack Rivers, 171

Who Will Build a Cottage?

I believe that there is an ideal or real nature, infinitely
more perfect than the actual as there is an ideal life of
man. Else where are the glorious summers which in vision sometimes visit my brain

When nature ceases to be supernatural to a man—
what will he do then? Of what worth is human life—if its
actions are no longer to have this sublime and unexplored scenery. Who will build a cottage and dwell in it
with enthusiasm if not in the elysian fields?

2 November 1843, *Journal* 1: 481

Nature, My Home

My home is as much of nature as my heart embraces, if I
only warm my house, then is that only my home. But if I
sympathize with the heats and colds—the sounds and silence of nature and share the repose and equanimity that
reigns around me in the fields then are they my house, as
much as if the kettle sang—and the faggots crackled, and
the clock ticked on the wall.

20 December 1840, *Journal* 1: 208

A Holiness As I Walk

In the sunshine and the crowing of cocks I feel an illimitable holiness, which makes me bless God and myself. The warm sun casts his incessant gift at my feet as I walk along — unfolding his yellow worlds —

7 February 1841, *Journal* 1: 255

The Grandeur of the Storm

It is the unexplored grandeur of the storm which keeps up the spirits of the traveller. When I contemplate hard and bare life in the woods, I find my last consolation in its untrivialness — Shipwreck is less distressing because the breakers do not trifle with us. We are resigned as long as we recognise the sober and solemn mystery of nature. The dripping mariner finds consolation and sympathy in the infinite sublimity of the storm — It is a moral force as well as he. With courage he can lay down his life on the strand, for it never turned a deaf ear to him — nor has he ever exhausted its sympathy.

19 February 1841, *Journal* 1: 269

An Elixir

In society you will not find health but in nature — You must converse much with the field and woods if you would imbibe such health into your mind and spirit as you covet for your body — Society is always diseased and the best is the sickest — There is no scent in it so wholsome as that of these pines — nor any fragrance so penetrating and restorative as that of everlasting in high pastures.

Without that our feet at least stood in the midst of nature all our faces would be pale and livid.

I should like to keep some book of natural history always by me as a sort of elixir — the reading of which would restore the tone of my system — and secure me true and cheerful views of life. For to the sick nature is sick but to the well a fountain of health. To the soul that contemplates some trait of natural beauty no harm nor disappointment can come. The doctrines of despair — of spiritual or political servitude — no priestcraft nor tyranny — was ever taught by such as drank in the harmony of nature

31 December 1841, *Journal* 1: 353-54

An Inexpressible Happiness

A mild summer sun shines over forest and lake — The earth looks as fair this morning as the valhalla of the gods — Indeed our spirits never go beyond nature. In the woods there is an inexpressible happiness —

15 November 1841, *Journal* 1: 343

A Peculiarly Wild Nature

I seem to see somewhat more of my own kith and kin in the lichens on the rocks than in any books   It does seem as if mine were a peculiarly wild nature — which so yearns toward all wildness —. I know of no redeeming qualities in me — but a sincere love for some things —And when I am reproved I have to fall back on to this ground.

15 December 1841, *Journal* 1: 344

Cackling Hens in the Barn

What is all nature and human life at this moment — what the scenery and vicinity of a human soul — but the song of an early sparrow from yonder fences — and the cackling hens in the barn — So for one while my destiny loiters within ear-shot of these sounds — The great busy dame nature is concerned to know how many eggs her hens lay.

20 March 1842, *Journal* 1: 384

Speaking for Nature

The scholar is not apt to make his most familiar experience come gracefully to the aid of his expression. Very few men can speak of Nature, for instance, with any truth. They overstep her modesty, somehow or other, and confer no favor. They do not speak a good word for her. Most cry better than they speak, and you can get more nature out of them by pinching than by addressing them. The surliness with which the wood-chopper speaks of his woods, handling them as indifferently as his axe, is better than the mealy-mouthed enthusiasm of the lover of nature.

"Sunday," *A Week on the Concord and Merrimack Rivers*, 108–9

Serving Nature

I feel slightly complimented when nature condescends to make use of me without my knowledge — as when I help scatter her seeds in my walk — or carry burs and cockles on my clothes from field to field — I feel as though I had done something for the commonweal, and were entitled to board and lodging. — I take such airs upon me as the boy who holds a horse for the circus company — whom all the spectators envy.

6 February 1841, *Journal* 1: 253

O Baker Farm!

As I was leaving the Irishman's roof after the rain, bending my steps again to the pond, my haste to catch pickerel, wading in retired meadows, in sloughs and bogholes, in forlorn and savage places, appeared for an instant trivial to me who had been sent to school and college; but as I ran down the hill toward the reddening west, with the rainbow over my shoulder, and some faint tinkling sounds borne to my ear through the cleansed air, from I know not what quarter, my Good Genius seemed to say, — Go fish and hunt far and wide day by day, — farther and wider, — and rest thee by many brooks and hearth-sides without misgiving. Remember thy Creator in the days of thy youth. Rise free from care before the dawn, and seek adventures. Let the noon find thee by other lakes, and the night overtake thee every where at home. There are no larger fields than these, no worthier games than may here be played. Grow wild according to thy nature, like these sedges and brakes, which will never become English hay. Let the thunder rumble; what if it threaten ruin to farmers' crops? that is not its errand to thee. Take shelter under the cloud, while they flee to carts and sheds. Let not to get a living be thy trade, but thy sport. Enjoy the land, but own it not. Through want of enterprise and faith men are where they are, buying and selling, and spending their lives like serfs.

O Baker Farm!

"Baker Farm," *Walden,* 207–8

Oxen, Furrows, and Bean-Fields: Agricultural Concord

The town of Concord, Massachusetts, is usually thought of as the home of minutemen and transcendentalists — the place where "the embattled farmers" launched America's war for political independence on April 19, 1775, and where Ralph Waldo Emerson and Henry David Thoreau, more than half a century later, waged their own struggles for intellectual independence, both for themselves as writers and for American culture as a whole. But in the late nineteenth century, Concord acquired a distinction it never possessed in the years when it was a seedbed of revolutionary scholars and soldiers. It became a leading center of agricultural improvement. Thanks to the coming of the railroad in 1844, Concord farmers played milkmen to the metropolis and branched out into market gardening and fruit raising as well. Concord was nursery to a popular new variety of grape, developed by a retired mechanic-turned-horticulturist named Ephraim Bull. And to crown its reputation, the town called the cultural capital of antebellum America by Stanley Elkins became the asparagus capital of the Gilded Age. Concord was, in short, a full participant in yet another revolution: the agricultural revolution that transformed the countryside of New England in the middle decades of the nineteenth century.

—Robert A. Gross

An Honorable Occupation

The farmer increases the extent of the habitable earth. He makes soil. This is an honorable occupation.

2 March 1852, *Journal* 4: 371

Rye

There are certain crops which give me the idea of bounty — of the *Alma* Natura — I mean the grains. Potatoes do not so fill the lap of earth. This rye excludes everything else & takes possession of the soil. The farmer says next year I will raise a crop of rye. & he proceeds to clear away the brush — & either plows it, or if it is too uneven or stoney — burns & harrows it only — & scatters the seed with faith — And all winter the earth keeps his secret — unless it did leak out somewhat in the fall, and in the spring this early green on the hill sides betrays him. When I see this luxuriant crop spreading far and wide in spite of rock & bushes and unevenness of ground, I can not help thinking that it must have been unexpected by the farmer himself — & regarded by him as a lucky accident for which to thank fortune. — This to reward a transient faith — the gods had given. As if he must have forgotten that he did it until he saw the waving grain inviting his sickle. A kind of pin-a-fore to Nature.

8 July 1851, *Journal* 3: 296

Bringing In the Cows

It snowed in the night of the 6th and the ground is now covered. our first snow 2 inches deep   A week ago I saw cows being driven home from pasture — Now they are kept at home. Here's an end to their grazing. The farmer improves this first slight snow to accomplish some pressing jobs — to move some particular rocks on a drag, or

the like— I perceive how quickly he has seized the opportunity. I see no tracks now of cows or men or boys beyond the edge of the wood—suddenly they are shut up
—the remote pastures & hills beyond the woods are now
closed to cows & cowherds aye & to cowards

8 December 1850, *Journal* 3: 161–62

A Wood Auction

The farmers are now carting out their manure—& re-
moving the muck-heaps from the shore of ponds where it
will be inaccessible in the winter. Or are doing their fall
plowing—which destroys many insects and mellows the
soil— I also see some pulling their turnips and even getting in corn which has been left out notwithstanding the
crows. Those who have wood to sell—as the weather
grows colder and people can better appreciate the value
of fuel, lot off their woods and advertise a wood-auction

15 November 1850, *Journal* 3: 140

Haying Is War

The farmers are just finishing their meadow haying (today is sunday)— Those who have early potatoes may be
digging them or doing any other job which the haying
has obliged them to postpone— For six weeks or more
this has been the farmer's work to shave the surface of the
fields & meadows clean. This is done all over the country
—the razor is passed over these parts of nature's face the
country over— A 13th labor which methinks would have
broken the backs of Hercules would have given him a
memorable sweat—accomplished with what sweating of
scythes & early & late—

I chance know one young man who has lost his life in
this seasons campaign by over doing— In haying time

some men take double wages & they are engaged long before in the spring. To shave all the fields & meadows of New England clean— If men did this but once & not every year — we should never hear the last of that labor — it would be more famous in each farmers case than Buonaparte's road over the Simplon. It has no other bulletin but the truthful farmer's almanac— Ask them where scythe snathes are made & sold & rifles too if it is not a real labor. In its very weapons & its passes it has the semblance of war. Mexico was won with less exertion & less true valor than are required to do one season's haying in New England— The former work was done by those who played truant and ran away from the latter.

Those Mexican's were mown down more easily than the summer's crop of grass in many a farmer's fields.

Is there not some work in New England men. This haying is no work for marines nor for deserters — nor for U S troops so called nor for Westpoint cadets — it would wilt them & they would desert. Have they not deserted? — every field is a battle field to the mower — a pitched battle too — and whole winrows of dead have covered it in the course of the season. Early & late the farmer has gone forth with his formidable scythe — weapon of time — Times weapon — & fought the ground inch by inch — It is the summer's enterprise. And if we were a more poetic people horns would be blowed to celebrate its completion — there might be a hay maker's day— New Englands peaceful battles —

17 August 1851, *Journal* 3: 370–71

Hens

And now at half past 10 o'clock I hear the cockrils crow in Hubbard's barns. — and morning is already antici-

pated. It is the feathered wakeful thought in us that antic-
ipates the following day. This sound is wonderfully exhil-
irating at all times. These birds are worth far more to me
for their crowing & cackling—than for their drumsticks
& eggs. How singular the connexion of the hen with
man, that she leaves her eggs in his barns always—she is
a domestic fowl though still a little shyish of him— I cannot looking at the whole as an experiment still and won-
dering that in each case it succeeds. There is no doubt at
last but hens may be kept—they will put there eggs in
your barn—by a tacit agreement— They will not wander far from your yard.

11 July 1851, *Journal 3:* 302

Beans

These beans have results which are not harvested by me.
Do they not grow for woodchucks partly? The ear of
wheat, (in Latin *spica,* obsoletely *speca,* from *spe,* hope,)
should not be the only hope of the husbandman; its ker-
nel or grain (*granum* from *gerendo,* bearing,) is not all
that it bears. How, then, can our harvest fail? Shall I not
rejoice also at the abundance of the weeds whose seeds
are the granary of the birds? It matters little comparatively whether the fields fill the farmer's barns. The true
husbandman will cease from anxiety, as the squirrels
manifest no concern whether the woods will bear chest-
nuts this year or not, and finish his labor with every day,
relinquishing all claim to the produce of his fields, and
sacrificing in his mind not only his first but his last fruits
also.

"The Bean-Field," *Walden,* 166

How I Envy You!

Friend Rice,

You say you are in the hay field: how I envy you! Methinks I see thee stretched at thy ease by the side of a fragrant rick with a mighty flagon in one hand, a cold slice in the other, and a most ravenous appetite to boot.

5 August 1836, Letter to Charles Wyatt Rice,
Correspondence, 8

Loads of Hay

It is interesting to see loads of hay coming down from the country now a days — (within a week) they make them very broad & low. They do not carry hay by RR yet. The spoils of up-country fields. A *Mt* of dried herbs. I had forgotten that there ever was so much grass as they prove. — And all these horses & oxen & cows thus are still fed on the last summer's grass which has been dried! They still roam in the meads.

8 February 1852, *Journal* 4: 335–36

A Rest

Found Hosmer carting out manure from under his barn to make room for the winter. He said he was tired of farming — he was too old. Quoted Webster as saying that he had never eaten the bread of idleness for a single day — and thought that Lord Brougham might have said as much with truth while he was in the opposition, — but he did not know that he could say as much of himself. However — he did not wish to be idle — he merely wished to rest.

29 September 1851, *Journal* 4: 110–11

Minot

Minot was telling me today that he used to know a man in Lincoln who had no floor to his barn but waited till the ground froze then swept it clean in his barn & threshed his grain on it

He also used to see men threshing their buck-wheat in the field where it grew — having just taken off the surface down to a hard pan.

Minot used the word "*gavel*" to describe a parcel of stalks cast on the ground to dry. His are good old English words and I am always sure to find them in the dictionary — though I never heard them before in my life.

I was admiring his corn stalks disposed about the barn to dry over or astride the braces & the timbers — of such a fresh clean & handsome green retaining their strength & nutritive properties so — unlike the gross & careless husbandry of speculating money-making farmers —. who suffer their stalks to remain out till they are dry & dingy & black as chips. Minot is perhaps the most poetical farmer — who most realizes to me the poetry of the farmer's life — that I know. He does nothing (with haste and drudgery —) but as if he loved it. He makes the most of his labor and takes infinite satisfaction in every part of it. He is not looking forward to the sale of his crops — or any pecuniary profit, but he is paid by the constant satisfaction which his labor yields him. He has not too much land to trouble him — too much work to do — no hired man nor boy. — but simply to amuse himself & live. He cares not so much to raise a large crop as to do his work well.

He knows every pin & nail in his barn. If another linter is to be floored he lets no hired man rob him of that amusement — but he goes slowly to the woods and at his leisure selects a pitch pine tree cuts it & hauls it or gets it hauled to the mill and so he knows the history of his barn-floor

Farming is an amusement which has lasted him longer than gunning or fishing — He is never in a hurry to get his garden planted & yet is always planted soon enough — & none in the town is kept so beautifully clean — He always prophecies a failure of the crops. — and yet is satisfied with what he gets. His barn-floor is fastened down with oak pins & he prefers them to iron spikes — which he says will rust & give way —

He handles & amuses himself with every ear of his corn crop as much as a child with its playthings — & so his small crop goes a great way. He might well cry if it were carried to market. The seed of weeds is no longer in his soil.

He loves to walk in a swamp in windy weather & hear the wind groan through the pines.

He keeps a cat in his barn to catch the mice. He indulges in no luxury of food or dress or furniture — yet he is not penurious but merely simple. If his sister dies before him he may have to go to the alms house in his old age — yet he is not poor — for he does not want riches.

He gets out of each manipulation in the farmers operations a fund of entertainment which the speculating drudge hardly knows.

With never failing rhumatism & trembling hands — he seems yet to enjoy perennial health. Though he never reads a book — since he had finished the Naval Monument — he speaks the best of English

4 October 1851, Journal 4: 116–18

A Certain Moral Worth

After having read various books on various subjects for some months I take up "a report on" [sic] Farms by a committee of Middlesex Husbandmen — and read of the number of acres of bog that some farmer has redeemed & the number of rods of stone wall that he has built — & the number of tons of hay he now cuts or of bushels of corn or potatoes he raises there — & I feel as if I had got my foot down on to the — solid & sunny earth — the basis of all philosophy — & poetry — & religion even — I have faith that the man who redeemed some acres of land the past summer redeemed also some parts of his character — I shall not expect to find him ever in the almshouse or the prison — He is in fact so far on his way to heaven. — When he took the farm there was not a grafted tree on it — & now he realizes some thing handsome from the sale of fruit — These — in the absence of other facts are evidence of a certain moral worth.

1 March 1852, *Journal* 4: 369

A Modern Epic

If anybody thinks a thought how sure we are to hear of it — though it be only a half thought or half a delusion it gets into newspapers and all the country rings with it —

But how much clearing of the land & plowing and planting & building of stone wall is done every summer — without being reported in the newspapers or in literature. Agricultural literature is not as extensive as the fields — & the farmer's almanac is never a big book. And yet I think that the History (or poetry) of one farm from a state of nature to the highest state of cultivation comes nearer to being the true subject of a modern epic than the

seige of Jerusalem or any such paltry & ridiculous re-
source to which some have thought men reduced.

2 March 1852, *Journal* 4: 370

The Cattle Show

As I pass along the streets of our village of Concord on
the day of our annual Cattle-Show, when it usually happens that the leaves of the elms and buttonwoods begin
first to strew the ground under the breath of the October
wind, the lively spirits in their sap seem to mount as high
as any plow-boy's let loose that day; and they lead my
thoughts away to the rustling woods, where the trees are
preparing for their winter campaign. This autumnal festi-
val, when men are gathered in crowds in the streets as
regularly and by as natural a law as the leaves cluster and
rustle by the way-side, is naturally associated in my mind
with the fall of the year. The low of cattle in the streets
sounds like a hoarse symphony or running base to the
rustling of the leaves. The wind goes hurrying down the
country, gleaning every loose straw that is left in the
fields, while every farmer lad too appears to scud before
it, — having donned his best pea-jacket and pepper and
salt waistcoat, his unbent trousers, outstanding rigging of
duck, or kersymere, or corduroy, and his furry hat withal,
— to country fairs and cattle-shows, to that Rome among
the villages where the treasures of the year are gathered.
All the land over they go leaping the fences with their
ʾgh idle palms, which have never learned to hang by
 sides, amid the low of calves and the bleating of
— Amos, Abner, Elnathan, Elbridge, —
ʾ steep pine-bearing mountains to the plain."
ʾ sons of earth every mother's son of them,

with their great hearty hearts rushing tumultuously in herds from spectacle to spectacle, as if fearful lest there should not be time between sun and sun to see them all, and the sun does not wait more than in haying time.

"Friday," *A Week on the Concord and Merrimack Rivers*, 336–37

The True Farmer

Most men find farming unprofitable — But there are some who can get their living any where If you set them down on a bare rock they will thrive there. The true farmer is to those who come after him & take the benefit of his improvements — like the lichen which plants itself on the bare rock & grows & thrives & cracks it and makes a vegetable mould to the garden vegetable which grows in it.

14 March 1852, *Journal* 4: 391

Neat Cattle

The red color of cattle also is agreeable in a landscape — or let them be what color they may-red-black-white — or mouse color — or spotted — all which I have seen this afternoon. The cows which confined to the barn or barn yard all winter, were covered with filth — after roaming in flowery pastures possess now clean & shining coats & the cowy odor is without alloy — Indeed they make such an impression of neatness (I think of a white cow spotted with red & her two sizeable calves of like color which I saw this afternoon) that one who was unacquainted with etymology might be excused if he gave a new signification to the word neat as applied to cattle —

23 June 1852, *Journal* 5: 127

Two Guilty Farmers

How hardy are cows that lie in the fog chewing the cud all night. They wake up with no stiffness in their limbs. They are indifferent to fogs as frogs to water—like hippopotami fitted are they to dwell ever on the river bank of this world—fitted to meadows & their vicissitudes. I see where in pastures of short firm turf they have pulled up the grass by the roots & it lies scattered in small tufts. (To anticipate a little when I return this way I find two farmers loading their cart with dirt—and they are so unmanly as to excuse themselves to me for working this Sunday morning—by saying—with a serious face that they are burying a cow—which died last night—after some month of sickness—which however they unthinkingly admit that they killed last night being the most convenient time for them—and I see that they are now putting more loads of soil over her body to save the manure— How often men will betray their sense of guilt and hence their actual guilt by their excuses—where no guilt necessarily was. I remarked that it must be cold for a cow lying in such fogs all night but one answered properly— "Well, I don't know how it may be with a sick cow, but it won't hurt a well crittur any.")

25 July 1852, *Journal* 5: 246

Bulls

Pleasant to go over the hills for there there is most air stirring—but you must look out for bulls in the pastures. Saw one here reclining in the shade amid the cows—his short sanguinary horns betrayed him & we gave him a wide berth for they are not to be reasoned with.

19 June 1852, *Journal* 5: 113

Agriculture Is a Good School

Pm to Anursnuck

Herbage is drying up — even weeds are wilted & the corn rolls. Agriculture is a good school in which to drill a man Successful farming admits of no idling. Now is the haying season — How active must these men be all the country over that they may get through this work in a season. A few spoiled windrows — all black and musty have taught them that they must make hay while the sun shines & get it in before it rains.

23 July 1852, Journal 5: 240

Farmer or Shipwright?

I am often reminded that the farmer living far inland has not thought of ploughs & carts alone — Here when getting his fuel he cuts the roots or limbs of some sturdier with reference to the uses it may serve in the construction of a ship. The farmer not only gets out wood to burn but ship timber. It was he who decided the destiny some mighty oak — that it should become the keel of a famous ship. It is he who says Ye shall become ships to plow the sea — when he says Ye shall become money to me. It is in the woods & in the farmer's yard that the vessel is first put upon the stocks. He burns the hewings in his ample fire-place — he teams the rest of *med-ford* with the same yokes that plow his fields. With bars & chains he clutches & binds to wheels — & with numerous yokes drags it over the hills to the nearest port. He learns as well as the engineer what hills are steep — what ground ascends — By repeated strains & restings on the terraces he at length surmounts every difficulty. Think of the difficulties which the farmer silently overcomes, who conveys the keel or mast of a man of war from his woods to the nearest port — which would have defied the skill of a tribe of savages to overcome!

Men's ignorance is made as useful as their knowledge. If one knew more he would admire less. In the winter how many farmers help build ships — where men grow up who never saw the ocean.

14 January 1853, *Journal* 5: 442–43

Cow Bells

The rattling of the tea-kettle below stairs reminds me of the cow bells I used to hear when berrying in the Great Fields many years ago — sounding distant and deep amid the birches That cheap piece of tinkling brass which the farmer hangs about the cow's neck — has been more to me than the tons of metal which are swung in the belfry.

4 April 1841, *Journal* 1: 296

A Hill Farm

My neighbor says that his hill-farm is poor stuff and "only fit to hold the world together" — He deserves that God should give him better for so brave a treating of his gifts — more than for repining or a dogged putting up therewith. It is a sort of stay, or gore, or gusset, — and he will not be blinded by modesty or gratitude, but sees it for what it is — Knowing his neighbors fertile land he calls his by its right name. But perhaps my farmer forgets, that his lean soil has sharpened his wits. It is good for some crops — And beside you see the heavens at a lesser angle from the hill than from the vale.

13 February 1841, *Journal* 1: 265

Dawn and to Market

Sep 9th 2 A M

I go by the farmers houses & barns standing there in the dim light under the trees, as if they lay at an immense distance or under a veil. The farmer & his oxen now all asleep. Not even a watch-dog awake. The human slumbers. There is less of man in the world.

The fog in the lowlands on the Corner road — is never still — It now advances & envelopes me as I stand to write these words — then clears away — with ever noiseless step — It covers the meadows like a web. I hear the clock strike 3 Now at the clayey bank. The light of orion's belt seems to show traces of the blue day through which it came to us — The sky at least is lighter on that side than in the west even about the moon. Even by night the sky is blue & not black for we see through the veil of night into the distant atmosphere of day. I see to the plains of the sun. Where the sun beams are revelling. The cricket's? song on the alders of the causeway not quite so loud at this hour as at evening. The moon is getting low. I hear a wagon cross on[e] of the bridges leading into the town. I see the moon-light at this hour on a different side of objects. I smell the ripe apples many rods off beyond the bridge. A sultry night — a thin coat is enough.

On the first top of Conantum — I hear the farmer harnessing his horse and starting for the distant market, but no man harnesses himself, and starts for worthier enterprises. — One cock crow imbodies the whole story of the farmer's life. The moon is now sinking into clouds in the horizon — I see the glowworms deep in the grass by the brook side in midst of Conantum — The moon shines dun & red. A solitary Whippoorwill sings.

The clock strikes 4.

A few dogs bark—a few more wagons start for market —their faint rattling heard in the distance— I hear my owl without a name.— The murmur of the slow approaching freight-train—as far off perchance as Waltham & one early bird.

9 September 1851, *Journal* 4: 63–64

Life of the Haymaker

When we withdraw a little from the village—and perceive how it is embosomed in nature—where perhaps its roofs are gleaming in the setting sun— We wonder if the life of its inhabitants might not also be thus natural and innocent reflecting the aspects of nature. We are apt to view again the life of the haymaker of such simplicity and innocence as his occupation Do not the gleaming crops—the verdant lawns—the springing groves—the flocks and herds—suggest what kind of a man the farmer should be?

14 August 1843, *Journal* 1: 458–59

Setting Out Peach Trees

Visited Sampson Wilder of Bolton. His method of setting out peach trees is as follows.

Dig a hole six feet square and two deep, and remove the earth—cover the bottom to the depth of six inches with lime and ashes in equal proportions, and upon this spread another layer of equal thickness of horn pairings —tips of horns—bones—and the like—then fill up with a compost of sod and strong animal manure—say four bushels of hog manure to a cart load of sod— Cover the tree—which should be budded at two years old—but slightly, and at the end of two years dig a trench round it

three feet from the tree and six inches deep, and fill it
with lime and ashes.

Rustling the Hay

Beside the direct & steady rain large drops fall from the
trees & dimple the water. Stopped in the Barn on the
Baker Farm. Sat in the dry meadow hay — where the mice
nest. To sit there rustling the hay just beyond reach of the
rain while the storm roars without — it suggested an inexpressible dry stillness — the quiet of the hay-mow in a
rainy day — such stacks of quiet & undisturbed thought
— when there is not even a cricket to stir in the hay. —
but all without is wet & tumultuous, & all within is dry &
quiet — O what reams of thought one might have here —
The crackling of the hay makes silence audible. It is so
deep a bed, it makes one dream to sit on it.

First Journey from Home

I sometimes see a neighbor or two united with their boys
& hired men to drive their cattle to some far off country
pasture, 50 or 60 miles distant in N Hampshire — early in
the morning with their sticks & dogs — It is a memorable
time with the farmers boys and frequently their first journey from home — The herdsman in some mt pasture is
expecting them. And then in the fall when they go up to
drive them back — they speculate as to whether Janet or
brindle will know them — I heard such a boy exclaim on
such an occasion when the calf of the spring returned a
heifer — as he stroked her side — she knows me father —
she knows me. —

A Farmer's Horn

I hear now, at five o'clock, from this hill, a farmer's horn calling his hands in from the field to an early tea. Heard afar by the walker, over the woods at this hour or at noon, bursting upon the stillness of the air, putting life into some portion of the horizon, this is one of the most suggestive and pleasing of the country sounds produced by man. I know not how far it is peculiar to New England or the United States. I hear two or three prolonged blasts, as I walking alone some sultry noon in midst of the still woods,—a sound which I know to be produced by human breath, the most sonorous parts of which alone reach me,—and I see in my mind the hired men and master dropping the implements of their labor in the field and wending their way with a sober satisfaction toward the house; I see the well-sweep rise and fall; I see the preparatory ablutions and the table laden with the smoking meal. It is a significant hum in a distant part of the hive. Often it tells me [the] time of day.

1 June 1853, *Journal* V: 212–13

The Haymakers

I find that we are now in the midst of meadow-haying season, and almost every meadow or section of a meadow has its band of half a dozen mowers and rakers, either bending to their manly work with regular and graceful motion or resting in the shade, while the boys are turning the grass to the sun. I passed as many as sixty or a hundred men thus at work to-day. They stick up a twig with the leaves on, on the river's brink, as a guide for the mowers, that they may not exceed the owner's bounds. I hear their scythes cronching the coarse weeds by the river's brink as I row near. The horse or oxen stand near at hand in the shade on the firm land, waiting to draw home a load anon. I see a platoon of three or four mowers, one behind the other, diagonally advancing with regular sweeps across the broad meadow and ever and anon standing to whet their scythes. Or else, having made several bouts, they are resting in the shade on the edge of the firm land. In one place I see one sturdy mower stretched on the ground amid his oxen in the shade of an oak, trying to sleep; or I see one wending far inland with a jug to some well-known spring....

Now Lee and his men are returning to their meadow-haying after dinner, and stop at the well under the black oak in the field. I too repair to the well when they are gone, and taste the flavor of black strap on the bucket's edge. As I return down-stream, I see the haymakers now raking with hand or horse rakes into long rows or loading, one on the load placing it and treading it down, while others fork it up to him; and others are gleaning with rakes after the forkers. All farmers are anxious to get their meadow-hay as soon as possible for fear the river will rise. On the 2d, Hagar told me he had done all his haying, having little or no meadow, and now the chief business was to kill weeds in the orchard, etc. Formerly they used to think they had nothing to do when the haying was done and might go a-fishing for three weeks.

5 August 1854, *Journal* VI: 422–24

Cyrus Hubbard

I see the old pale-faced farmer out again on his sled now for the five-thousandth time, — Cyrus Hubbard, a man of a certain New England probity and worth, immortal and natural, like a natural product, like the sweetness of a nut, like the toughness of hickory. He, too, is a redeemer for me. How superior actually to the faith he professes! He is not an office-seeker. What an institution, what a revelation is a man! We are wont foolishly to think that the creed which a man professes is more significant than the fact he is. It matters not how hard the conditions seemed, how mean the world, for a man is a prevalent force and a new law himself. He is a system whose law is to be observed. The old farmer condescends to countenance still this nature and order of things. It is a great encouragement that an honest man makes this world his abode. He rides on the sled drawn by oxen, world-wise, yet comparatively so young, as if they had seen scores of winters. The farmer spoke to me, I can swear, clean, cold, moderate as the snow. He does not melt the snow where he treads. Yet what a faint impression that encounter may make on me after all! Moderate, natural, true, as if he were made of earth, stone, wood, snow. I thus meet in this universe kindred of mine, composed of these elements.

1 December 1856, *Journal* IX: 144–45

Webster's Large Farm

After taking the road by Webster's beyond South Marshfield I walked a long way at noon hot & thirsty before I could find a suitable place to sit & eat my dinner — a place where the shade & the sward pleased me. At length I was obliged to put up with a small shade close to the ruts where the only stream I had seen for some time crossed the road. Here also numerous robins came to cool & wash themselves & to drink. They stood in the water up to their bellies from time to time wetting their wings & tails & also ducking their heads & sprinkling the water over themselves — then they sat on a fence near by to dry. Then a goldfinch came & did the same accompanied by the less brilliant female. These birds evidently enjoyed their bath greatly. — & it seemed indispensable to them.

A neighbor of Websters told me that he had hard onto 1600 acres & was still buying more — a farm & factory within the year — cultivated 150 acres — I saw 12 acres of potatoes together — the same of rye & wheat & more methinks of buck wheat. 15 or 16 men Irish mostly at 10 dollars a month doing the work of 50 with a yankee overseer long a resident of Marshfield named Wright. Would eat only the produce of his farm during the few weeks he was at home — brown bread & butter — & milk — & sent out for a pig's cheek to eat with his greens — ate only what grew on his farm but drank more than ran on his farm

Begin by Burning Fences:
The Seeds of Conservation

Flowage, in the legal sense, means flooding, as by a dam. And it was the dam at Billerica, on the Concord, first erected to provide waterpower and later heightened to increase the flow into the Middlesex Canal, that destroyed the meadows, for the level of both the Concord and the Sudbury rivers rose behind it, flooding the grasslands as far upstream as Farm Bridge at Pelham Island. The resulting legal action, after half a century of complaints, produced one of the historic confrontations of the time. It pitted the power of industrial expansion against the embattled farmers. Some of the most distinguished jurists of the East appeared in the case, and Henry Thoreau, as the leading surveyor in Concord, was employed by the River Meadow Association to collect facts about the depth of the rivers and their rise and fall, for use by the lawyers representing the farmers.

— Edwin Way Teale

Begin by Burning Fences

Nowadays almost all man's improvements, so called, as the building of houses, and the cutting down of the forest and of all large trees, simply deform the landscape, and make it more and more tame and cheap. A people who would begin by burning the fences and let the forest stand! I saw the fences half consumed, their ends lost in the middle of the prairie, and some worldly miser with a surveyor looking after his bounds, while heaven had taken place around him, and he did not see the angels going to and fro, but was looking for an old post-hole in the midst of paradise. I looked again, and saw him standing in the middle of a boggy, stygian fen, surrounded by devils, and he had found his bounds without a doubt, three little stones, where a stake had been driven, and looking nearer, I saw that the Prince of Darkness was his surveyor.

"Walking," 100

They Cannot Injure Walden

They cannot fatally injure Walden with an axe, for they have done their worst & failed.

1 September 1852, *Journal* 5: 332

Wild Apples

The era of wild apples will soon be over— I wander through old orchards of great extent now all gone to decay all of native fruit which for the most part went to the cider mill— But since the temperance reform—and the general introduction of grafted fruit—no wild apples such as I see every where in deserted pastures and where the woods have grown up among them—are set out. I fear that he who walks over these hills a century hence will not know the pleasure of knocking off wild apples— Ah poor man! there are many pleasures which he will be debarred from. Notwithstanding the prevalence of the Baldwin & the porter, I doubt if as extensive orchards are set out to day in this town as there were a century ago when these vast straggling cider orchards were set out. Men stuck in a tree then by every wall side & let it take its chance— I see nobody planting trees today in such out of the way places along almost every road & lane & wall side, and at the bottom of dells in the wood. Now that they have grafted trees & pay a price for them they collect them into a plot by their houses & fence them in.

16 November 1850, *Journal* 3: 143

I Wish to Speak a Word for Nature

I wish to speak a word for nature, for absolute freedom and wildness, as contrasted with a freedom and culture merely civil,— to regard man as an inhabitant, or a part and parcel of Nature, rather than a member of society. I wish to make an extreme statement, if so I may make an emphatic one, for there are enough champions of civilization: the minister, and the school-committee, and every one of you will take care of that.

"Walking," 93

Comparatively Degenerate Days

To preserve wild animals implies generally the creation of a forest for them to dwell in or resort to. So it is with man. A hundred years ago they sold bark in our streets peeled from our own woods. In the very aspect of those primitive and rugged trees, there was, methinks, a tanning principle which hardened and consolidated the fibres of men's thoughts. Ah! Already I shudder for these comparatively degenerate days of my native village, when you cannot collect a load of bark of good thickness,— and we no longer produce tar and turpentine.

The civilized nations—Greece, Rome, England—

have been sustained by the primitive forests which anciently rotted where they stand. They survive as long as the soil is not exhausted. Alas for human culture! little is to be expected of a nation, when the vegetable mould is exhausted, and it is compelled to make manure of the bones of its fathers. There the poet sustains himself merely by his own superfluous fat, and the philosopher comes down on his marrow-bones.

"Walking," 117

What Is the Use of a House?

Men and boys are learning all kinds of trades but how to make *men* of themselves. They learn to make houses, but they are not so well housed, they are not so contented in their houses, as the woodchucks in their holes. What is the use of a house if you haven't got a tolerable planet to put it on?

20 May 1860, Letter to H. G. O. Blake,
Correspondence, 578

How Long Will These Woods Last?

What is it that I see from a mile to a mile & a half & 2 miles distant in the horizon on all sides of our villages — the woods. — which still almost without exception encircle the towns. — They at least bound almost every view. They have been driven off only so far. Where still wild creatures haunt. How long will these last? Is this a universal and permanent feature? Is it not an interesting, and important question whether these are decreasing or not. Have the oldest countries retained it?

Look out what window I will my eyes rest in the distance on a forest! Is this fact of no significance— Is this circumstance of no value? Why such pains in old countries to plant gardens & parks? — A certain sample of wild nature — a certain primitiveness.

22 January 1852, *Journal* 4: 275–76

The Death of a Noble Tree

This afternoon being on Fair Haven Hill I heard the sound of a saw — and soon after from the cliff saw two men sawing down a noble pine beneath about 40 rods off. I resolved to watch it till it fell — the last of a dozen or more which were left when the forest was cut and for 15 years have waved in solitary majesty over the sproutland. I saw them like beavers or insects gnawing at the trunk of this noble tree, the diminutive mannikins with their crosscut saw which could scarcely span it. It towered up a hundred feet as I afterward found by measurement — one of the tallest probably now in the township & straight as an arrow, but slanting a little toward the hill side. — its top seen against the frozen river & the hills of Conantum. I watch closely to see when it begins to move. Now the sawers stop — and with an axe open it a little on the side toward which it leans that it may break the faster. And now their saw goes again

— Now surely it is going — it is inclined one quarter of the quadrant, and breathless I expect its crashing fall — But no I was mistaken it has not moved an inch, it stands at the same angle as at first. It is 15 minutes yet to its fall. Still its branches wave in the wind as if it were destined to stand for a century, and the wind soughs through its needles as of yore; it is still a forest tree — the most majestic tree that waves over Musketaquid. — The silvery sheen of the sunlight is reflected from its needles — it still affords an inaccessible crotch for the squirrel's nest — not a lichen has forsaken its mastlike stem — — its raking mast — the hill is the hull. Now, now's the moment — the mannikins at its base are fleeing from their crime — they have dropped the guilty saw & axe. How slowly & majestically it starts — as if it were only swayed by a summer breeze and would return without a sigh to its location in the air — & now it fans the hill side with its fall and it lies down to its bed in the valley from which it is never to rise, as softly as a feather, folding its green mantle about it like a warrior — as if tired of standing it embraced the earth with silent joy.

— returning its elements to the dust again — but hark! there you only saw — but did not hear — There now comes a deafening crash to these rocks

— advertising you that even trees do not die without a groan. It rushes to embrace the earth, & mingle its elements with the dust. And now all is still once more & forever both to eye & ear.

I went down and measured it. It was about 4 feet in diameter where it was sawed — about 100 feet long. Before I had reached it — the axemen had already half divested it of its branches. Its gracefully spreading top was a perfect wreck on the hill side as if it had been made of glass — & the tender cones of one years growth upon its summit appealed in vain & too late to the mercy of the chopper. Already he has measured it with his axe — and marked out the mill logs it will make. And the space it occupied in upper air is vacant for the next 2 centuries. It is lumber He has laid waste the air. When the fish hawk in the spring revisits the banks of the Musketaquid, he will circle in vain to find his accustomed perch. — & the hen-hawk will mourn for the pines lofty enough to protect her brood. A plant which it has taken two centuries to perfect rising by slow stages into the heavens — has this afternoon ceased to exist. Its sapling top had expanded to this January thaw as the forerunner of summers to come. Why does not not the village bell sound a knell. I hear no knell tolled — I see no procession of mourners in the streets — or the woodland aisles — The squirrel has leapt to another tree — the hawk has circled further off — & has now settled upon a new eyre but the woodman is preparing lay his axe at the root of that also.

30 December 1851, *Journal* 4: 227–29

They Are Cutting Down Our Woods

This winter they are cutting down our woods more seriously than ever — Fair Haven Hill — Walden — Linnaea Borealis wood &c &c Thank God they cannot cut down the clouds.

21 January 1852, *Journal* 4: 273

The Axe Can Deprive Me of Much

I see in the woods the woodsman's embers — which have melted a circular hole in the snow — where he warms his coffee. at noon. But these days the fire does not melt the snow over a space 3 feet across.

These woods! why do I not feel their being cut more sorely? Does it not affect me nearly? The axe can deprive me of much. Concord is sheared of its pride. I am certainly the less attached to my native town in consequence. One & a main link is broken. I shall go to Walden less frequently.

24 January 1852, *Journal* 4: 283

The Vestibule of Nature

The future will no doubt be a more natural life than this. We shall be acquainted and shall use flowers and stars, and sun and moon, and occupy this nature which now stands over and around us. We shall reach up to the stars and pluck fruit from many parts of the universe. We shall purely use the earth and not abuse it— God is in the breeze and whispering leaves and we shall then hear him. We live in the midst of all the beauty and grandeur that was ever described or conceived.

We have already entered the vestibule of Nature. It was here be assured under these heavens that the gods intended our immortal life should pass—these stars were set to adorn and light it—these flowers to carpet it

26 August 1843, *Journal* 1: 460

Squares & Triangles

In the woods one bough relieves another, and we look into them, not with strained, but relaxed, eyes. Seeing has a holiday in their maze. — But as soon as man comes into nature, by running counter to her, and cutting her off where she was continuous, he makes her angular and formal, and when we would bathe our eyes in the prospect it only makes them ache.

I saw today where some pines had been felled at various angles with the rest of the wood, and on that side nature offended me, as a diagram. It seemed as if man could not lay his tree gracefully along the earth as the wind does, but my eye as well as the squirrel's would detect it. I saw squares and triangles only.

15 December 1840, *Journal* 1: 203–4

Fresh Wounds

Hardly a rood of land but can show its fresh wound or indelible scar, in proof that earlier or later man has been there.

14 March 1838, *Journal* 1: 36

Forest Fires

I have often remarked with how much more comfort & pleasure I could walk in wood through which a fire had run the previous year. It will clean the forest floor like a broom—perfectly smooth & clear—no twigs left to crackle under foot—the dead & rotten wood removed & thus in the course of 2 or 3 years new huckleberry fields are created for the town—for birds & men.

When the lightning burns the forest its director makes no apology to man—and I was but his agent. Perhaps we owe to this accident partly some of the noblest natural parks. It is inspiriting to walk amid the fresh green sprouts of grass & shrubbery pushing upward through the charred surface with more vigorous growth

1 July 1850, *Journal* 3: 91

Wild Meadows

I should be glad if all the meadows on the earth were left in a wild state, if that were the consequence of men's beginning to redeem themselves.

"Baker Farm," *Walden,* 205

Destruction of the Fishery

Salmon, Shad, and Alewives, were formerly abundant here, and taken in weirs by the Indians, who taught this method to the whites, by whom they were used as food and as manure, until the dam, and afterward the canal at Billerica, and the factories at Lowell, put an end to their migrations hitherward; though it is thought that a few more enterprising shad may still occasionally be seen in this part of the river. It is said, to account for the destruction of the fishery, that those who at that time represented the interests of the fishermen and the fishes, remembering between what dates they were accustomed to take the grown shad, stipulated, that the dams should be left open for that season only, and the fry, which go down a month later, were consequently stopped and destroyed by myriads. Others say that the fishways were not properly constructed. Perchance, after a few thousands of years, if the fishes will be patient, and pass their summers elsewhere, meanwhile, nature will have levelled the Billerica dam, and the Lowell factories, and the Grass-ground River run clear again, to be explored by new migratory shoals, even as far as the Hopkinton pond and Westborough swamp.

"Saturday," *A Week on the Concord and Merrimack Rivers*, 33–34

The Fur Trade

What a pitiful business is the fur trade, which has been pursued now for so many ages, for so many years by famous companies which enjoy a profitable monopoly and control a large portion of the earth's surface, unweariedly pursuing and ferreting out small animals by the aid of all the loafing class tempted by rum and money, that you may rob some little fellow-creature of its coat to adorn or thicken your own, that you may get a fashionable covering in which to hide your head, or a suitable robe in which to dispense justice to your fellow-men! Regarded from the philosopher's point of view, it is precisely on a level with rag and bone picking in the streets of the cities. The Indian led a more respectable life before he was tempted to debase himself so much by the white man. Think how many musquash and weasel skins the Hudson's Bay Company pile up annually in their warehouses, leaving the bare red carcasses on the banks of the streams throughout all British America, — and this it is, chiefly, which makes it *British* America. It is the place where Great Britain goes a-mousing. We have heard much of the wonderful intelligence of the beaver, but that regard for the beaver is all a pretense, and we would give more for a beaver hat than to preserve the intelligence of the whole race of beavers.

When we see men and boys spend their time shooting and trapping musquash and mink, we cannot but have a poorer opinion of them, unless we thought meanly of them before. Yet the world is imposed on by the fame of the Hudson's Bay and Northwest Fur Companies, who are only so many partners more or less in the same sort of business, with thousands of just such loafing men and boys in their service to abet them. On the one side is the Hudson's Bay Company, on the other the company of scavengers who clear the sewers of Paris of their vermin. There is a good excuse for smoking out or poisoning rats which infest the house, but when they are as far off as Hudson's Bay, I think that we had better let them alone. To such an extent do time and distance, and our imaginations, consecrate at last not only the most ordinary, but even vilest pursuits. The efforts of legislation from time to time to stem the torrent are significant as showing that there is some sense and conscience left, but they are insignificant in their effects. We will fine Abner if he shoots a singing bird, but encourage the army of Abners that compose the Hudson's Bay Company.

An Emasculated Country

I spend a considerable portion of my time observing the habits of the wild animals, my brute neighbors. By their various movements and migrations they fetch the year about to me. Very significant are the flight of geese and the migration of suckers, etc., etc. But when I consider that the nobler animals have been exterminated here,— the cougar, panther, lynx, wolverene, wolf, bear, moose, deer, the beaver, the turkey, etc., etc.,— I cannot but feel as if I lived in a tamed, and, as it were, emasculated country. Would not the motions of those larger and wilder animals have been more significant still? Is it not a maimed and imperfect nature that I am conversant with? As if I were to study a tribe of Indians that had lost all its warriors. Do not the forest and the meadow now lack expression, now that I never see nor think of the moose with the lesser forest on his head in the one, nor of the beaver in the other? When I think what were the various sounds and notes, the migrations and works, and changes of fur and plumage which ushered in the spring and marked the other seasons of the year, I am reminded that this my life in nature, this particular round of natural phenomena which I call a year, is lamentably incomplete.

Why Not a Forest & Huckleberry-field?

Each town should have a park, or rather a primitive forest, of five hundred or a thousand acres, where a stick should never be cut for fuel, a common possession for-

ever, for instruction and recreation. We hear of cow-com-
mons and ministerial lots, but we want *men*-commons
and lay-lots, inalienable forever. Let us keep the New
World *new,* preserve all the advantages of living in the
country. There is meadow and pasture and wood-lot for
the town's poor. Why not a forest and huckleberry-field
for the town's rich? All Walden Wood might have been
preserved for our park forever, with Walden in its midst,
and the Easterbrooks Country, an unoccupied area of
some four square miles, might have been our huckleberry-field. If any owners of these tracts are about to leave
the world without natural heirs who need or deserve to
be specially remembered, they will do wisely to abandon
their possession to all, and not will them to some individual who perhaps has enough already. As some give to
Harvard College or another institution, why might not
another give a forest or huckleberry-field to Concord? A
town is an institution which deserves to be remembered.
We boast of our system of education, but why stop at
schoolmasters and schoolhouses? We are all schoolmasters, and our schoolhouse is the universe. To attend
chiefly to the desk or schoolhouse while we neglect the
scenery in which it is placed is absurd. If we do not look
out we shall find our fine schoolhouse standing in a cow-
yard at last.

15 October 1859, *Journal* XII: 387

Protecting Birds

When the question of the protection of birds comes up,
the legislatures regard only a low use and never a high
use; the best-disposed legislators employ one, perchance, only to examine their crops and see how many

grubs or cherries they contain, and never to study their dispositions, or the beauty of their plumage, or listen and report on the sweetness of their song. The legislature will preserve a bird professedly not because it is a beautiful creature, but because it is a good scavenger or the like. This, at least, is the defense set up. It is as if the question were whether some celebrated singer of the human race — some Jenny Lind or another — did more harm or good, should be destroyed, or not, and therefore a committee should be appointed, not to listen to her singing at all, but to examine the contents of her stomach and see if she devoured anything which was injurious to the farmers and gardeners, or which they cannot spare.

8 April 1859, *Journal* XII: 124–25

Our Museum

We cut down the few old oaks which witnessed the transfer of the township from the Indian to the white man, and commence our museum with a cartridge-box taken from a British soldier in 1775!

3 January 1861, *Journal* XIV: 307

Thank God, Men Can't Fly

It would be worth the while if in each town there were a committee appointed to see that the beauty of the town received no detriment. If we have the largest boulder in the county, then it should not belong to an individual, nor be made into door-steps.

As in many countries precious metals belong to the crown, so here more precious natural objects of rare beauty should belong to the public.

Not only the channel but one or both banks of every

river should be a public highway. The only use of a river is not to float on it.

Think of a mountain-top in the township — even to the minds of the Indians a sacred place — only accessible through private grounds! a temple, as it were, which you cannot enter except by trespassing and at the risk of letting out or letting in somebody's cattle! in fact the temple itself in this case private property and standing in a man's cow-yard, — for such is commonly the case.

New Hampshire courts have lately been deciding — as if it was for them to decide — whether the top of Mt. Washington belonged to A or to B; and, it being decided in favor of B, as I hear, he went up one winter with the proper officer and took formal possession of it. But I think that the top of Mt. Washington should not be private property; it should be left unappropriated for modesty and reverence's sake, or if only to suggest that earth has higher uses than we put her to. I know it is a mere figure of speech to talk about temples nowadays, when men recognize none, and, indeed, associate the world with heathenism....

But most men, it seems to me, do not care for Nature and would sell their share in all her beauty, as long as they may live, for a stated sum — many for a glass of rum. Thank God, men cannot as yet fly, and lay waste the sky as well as the earth! We are safe on that side for the present.

The Place to Which the Roads Tend: The Growth of Community

In 1846, descendants of [the] founding families and of those who "fired the shot heard round the world" were still tilling the fields originally cleared and later defended by their forebears. A farming community, yes—but one in transition. The industrial revolution was in full swing. Produce from the rich soil of the Midwest was flooding eastern markets. A recently completed railroad had linked Concord with Boston; it was at once a threat to the farmer's traditional means of livelihood and a stimulus to intellectual achievement.... It was a time when people's consciences were troubled, when utopian communities were seeking an alternative to growing materialism, when the drive for conquest of the continent was reaching white heat, when the issue of slavery threatened to divide the nation, when violence loomed ahead. Yet the response of this quiet New England town was one of hope rather than despair.

— Paul Brooks

Villages

The village is the place to which the roads tend, a sort of expansion of the highway, as a lake of a river. It is the body of which roads are the arms and legs,—a trivial or quadrivial place, the thoroughfare and ordinary of travellers. The word is from the Latin *villa,* which, together with *via,* a way, or more anciently *ved* and *vella,* Varro derives from *veho,* to carry, because the villa is the place to and from which things are carried. They who got their living by teaming were said *vellaturam facere.* Hence, too, apparently, the Latin word *vilis* and our vile; also *villain.* This suggests what kind of degeneracy villagers are liable to. They are wayworn by the travel that goes by and over them, without travelling themselves.

"Walking," 101–2

Trespassing

I trust that the walkers of the present day are conscious of the blessings which they enjoy in the comparative freedom with which they can ramble over the country & enjoy the landscape — anticipating with compassion that future day when possibly it will be partitioned off into so called pleasure grounds where only a few may enjoy the narrow & exclusive pleasure which is compatible with ownership. When walking over the surface of Gods earth — shall be construed to mean trespassing on some gentleman's grounds. When fences shall be multiplied & man traps & other engines invented to confine men to the public road. I am thankfull that we have yet so much room in America.

12 February 1851, *Journal* 3: 189–90

An Old Meandering Road

July 21st 8 AM

The forenoon is fuller of light. The butterflies on the flowers look like other & frequently larger flowers themselves. Now I yearn for one of those old meandering dry uninhabited roads which lead away from towns — which lead us away from temptation, which conduct to the outside of earth — over its uppermost crust — where you may forget in what country you are travelling — where no farmer can complain that you are treading down his grass — no gentleman who has recently constructed a seat in the country that you are trespassing — on which you can go off at half cock — and waive adieu to the village — along which you may travel like a pilgrim — going nowhither. Where travellers are not too often to be met. Where my spirit is free — where the walls & fences are not cared for — where your head is more in heaven than your feet are on earth — which have long reaches — where you can see the approaching traveller half a mile off and be prepared for him — not so luxuriant a soil as to attract men — some root and stump fences which do not need attention — Where travellers have no occasion to stop — but pass along and leave you to your thoughts — Where it makes no odds which way you face whether you are going or coming — whether it is morning or evening — mid noon or mid-night — Where earth is cheap enough by being public. Where you can walk and think with least obstruction — there being nothing to measure progress by. Where you can pace when your breast is full and cherish your moodiness. Where you are not in false relations with men — are not dining nor conversing with them. By which you may go to the uttermost parts of the earth —

21 July 1851, *Journal* 3: 317–18

I Can Easily Walk

I can easily walk ten, fifteen, twenty, any number of miles, commencing at my own door, without going by any house, without crossing a road except where the fox and the mink do: first along by the river, and then the brook, and then the meadow and the woodside. There are square miles in my vicinity which have no inhabitant. From many a hill I can see civilization and the abodes of man afar. The farmers and their works are scarcely more obvious than woodchucks and their burrows. Man and his affairs, church and state and school, trade and commerce, and manufactures and agriculture, even politics, the most alarming of them all, — I am pleased to see how little space they occupy in the landscape. Politics is but a narrow field, and that still narrower highway yonder leads to it. I sometimes direct the traveller thither. If you would go to the political world, follow the great road, — follow that market-man, keep his dust in your eyes, and it will lead you straight to it; for it, too, has its place merely, and does not occupy all space. I pass from it as from a bean-field into the forest, and it is forgotten. In one half-hour I can walk off to some portion of the earth's surface where a man does not stand from one year's end to another, and there, consequently, politics are not, for they are but as the cigar-smoke of a man.

"Walking," 100–101

The Telegraph Comes to Concord

In a day or two the first message will be conveyed or transmitted over the magnetic telegraph through this town — as a thought traverses space — and no citizen of the town shall be aware of it. The atmosphere is full of telegraphs equally unobserved.

2 September 1851, *Journal* 4: 28

Like a Harp

As I went under the new telegraph wire I heard it vibrating like a harp high over head. — it was as the sound of a far off glorious life a supernal life which came down to us. — and vibrated the lattice work of this life of ours.

3 September 1851, *Journal* 4: 35

The Telegraph harp has spoken to me more distinctly and effectually than any man ever did.

15 March 1852, *Journal* 4: 389

Old Hosmer

Old Mr. Joseph Hosmer who helped me to-day — said that he used to know all about the lots — but since they've chopped off so much & the woods have grown up — he finds himself lost. 30 or 40 years ago when he went to meeting he knew every face in the meeting house — even the boys & girls looked so much like their parents — but after 10 or 12 years they would have outgrown his knowledge entirely (they would have altered so — but he knew the old folks still — because they held their own & did'nt alter. Just so he could tell the boundaries of the old wood which had'nt been cut down, but the young wood altered so much in a few years, that he could'nt tell anything about it.

When I asked him why the old road which went by this swamp was so round about, he said he would answer me as Mr ––– did him in a similar case once Why if they had made it straight they would'nt have left any room for improvement.

19 November 1851, *Journal* 4: 193–94

Unsettled Farmers

The rail-roads as much as anything appear to have unsettled the farmers. Our young Concord farmers & their young wives hearing this bustle about them — seeing the world all going by as it were — some daily to the cities about their business, some to California — plainly cannot make up their minds to live the quiet retired old-fashioned country-farmer's life — They are impatient if they live more than a mile from a railroad. While all their neighbors are rushing to the road — there are few who have character or bravery enough to live off the road. He is too well aware what is going on in the world not to wish to take some part in it.

28 September 1851, *Journal* 4: 108–9

Few Nuts Now

Minot shells all his corn by hand. He has got a box full ready for the mill. He will not winnow it for he says the chaff? makes it lie loose & dry faster. He tells me that Jacob Baker who raises as fair corn as anybody — gives all the corn of his own raising to his stock — & buys the flat yellow corn of the South for bread — & yet the northern corn is worth the most per bushel

Minot did not like this kind of farming any better than I — Baker also buys a great quantity of "Shorts" below for his cows — to make more milk.

He remembers when a Prescott who lived where E. Hosmer does used to let his hogs run in the woods in the fall — and they grew quite fat on the acorns &c they found, but now there are few nuts & it is against the law.

He tells me of the places in the woods which to his eyes are unchanged since he was a boy — as natural as life—he tells me then that in some respects he is still a boy. & yet the grey-squirrels were 10 then to 1 now. But for the most part he says the world is turned upside down.

The Acton Monument

The new monument in Acton rising by the side of its *mt* houses like a tall & slender chimney looking black against the sky—!! I cannot associate that tall & slender column or any column in fact with the death of Davis & Hosmer—& Concord fight & the Am. revolution. It should have been a large flat stone rather covered with lichens—like an old farmer's door step which it took all the oxen in the town to draw——Such a column this as might fitly stand perchance in Abysinia or Nubia but not here in middlsex Co— where the genius of the people does not soar after that fashion. It is the Acton flue. to dissipate the vapors of patriotism in the upper air— which confined would be deleterious to animal and vegetable health. The Davis & Hosmer Monument might have been a doorstep to the Town House.

A Deserted Country

Old Mr. Joseph Hosmer, who lives where Hadley did— remembers when there were two or three times as many inhabitants in that part of the town as there are now— A blacksmith with his shop in front where he now lives—a Goldsmith (Oliver Wheeler?) at the fork in the road just beyond him, one *in front* of Tarbel's—one in the orchard on the S side of the lane in front of Tarbel's—one

further Nathan Wheeler on the right of the old road by
the Balm of Gilead— 3 between Tarbel's & J P Brown's,
a tavern at Lorings—a store at The Dodge cottage that
was burnt also at Derbey's?—&c &c The farms were
smaller then— One man now often holds 2 or 3 old
farms. We walk in a deserted country.

21 November 1851, Journal 4: 196

A Place of Business

This world is a place of business—what an infinite bustle. I am awaked almost every night by the panting of the
steam-engine. It interrupts my dreams. There is no Sabbath— It would be glorious to see mankind at leisure for
once.

4 March 1852, Journal 4: 373

The Railroad

The RR men have now their hands full— I hear & see
blue-birds come with the warm wind. The sand is flowing in the deep cut— I am affected by the sight of the
moist red sand or subsoil under the edge of the sandy
bank—under the pitch pines. The r-road is perhaps our
pleasantest & wildest roads. It only makes deep cuts into
& through the hills—on it are no houses nor foot travellers. The travel on it does not disturb me. The woods
are left to hang over it

— Though straight is wild in its accompaniments—
all is raw edges. Even the laborers on it are not like other
laborers— Its houses if any are shanties—& its ruins the
ruins of shanties shells where the race that built the R R
dwelt—& the bones they gnawed lie about. I am cheered
by the sound of running water now down the wooden

troughs on each side of the cut. Then it is the dryest walking in wet weather & the easiest in snowy. This road breaks the surface of the earth. Even the sight — of smoke from the shanty excites me today. Already these puddles on the RR reflecting the pine woods remind me of summer lakes

9 March 1852, *Journal* 4: 382–83

Hopeful Young America?

Mill Road S of Ministerial Swamp 3 P.m. As I stand under the hill beyond J. Hosmer's — and look over the plains westward toward Acton — & see the farm houses nearly half a mile apart — few & solitary — in these great fields between these stretching woods — out of the world — where the children have to go far to school — the still stagnant — heartening — life — everlasting & gone-to-seed country — so far from the post Office where the weekly paper comes — Wherein the new-married wife cannot live for loneliness — And the young man has to depend upon his horse — — See young J Hosmer's House whither he returns with his wife in despair — after living in the City. I standing in Tarbells' road which he alone cannot break out. The world in winter for most walkers reduced to a sled track winding far through drifts All springs ceiled up & no digressions Where the old man thinks he may possibly afford to rust it out not having long to live — but the young man pines to get nearer the P.O. & the Lyceum. Is restless — & resolves to go to California, because the Depot is a mile off.

— Where rabbits & partridges multiply & muskrats are more numerous than ever. — And none of the farmer's sons are willing to be farmers — And the apple trees are decayed — & the cellar holes are more numerous than the houses — And the old maids — wish to sell out & move into the vilage — & have waited 20 years in vain for this purpose — & never finished but one room in the house — Lands of which the Indian was long since dispossessed — and now the farms are run out — & what were forests are grain fields — & what were grain-fields — pastures — Dwellings which only those Arnolds those Coureurs de bois the baker & the butcher visit — to which at least the latter penetrates for the annual calf — & as he returns the cow lows after — Whither the village never penetrates but in huckleberry time perchance — & if he does not who does? Where the owls are a regular serenade.. — I say standing there & seeing these things, I cannot realize that this is that hopeful young America which is famous throughout the world — for its activity & enterprise — & this is the most thickly settled & Yankee part of it.

27 January 1852, *Journal* 4: 294–96

See This River

Unfitted to some extent for the purposes of commerce by the sand-bar at its mouth, see how this river was devoted from the first to the service of manufactures. Issuing from the iron region of Franconia, and flowing through still uncut forests, by inexhaustible ledges of granite, with Squam, and Winnepisiogee, and Newfound, and Massabesic Lakes for its mill-ponds, it falls over a succession of natural dams, where it has been offering its *privileges* in vain for ages, until at last the Yankee race came to *improve* them. Standing at its mouth, look up its sparkling stream to its source, — a silver cascade which falls all the way from the White Mountains to the sea, — and behold a city on each successive plateau, a busy colony of human beaver around every fall. Not to mention Newburyport and Haverhill, see Lawrence, and Lowell, and Nashua, and Manchester, and Concord, gleaming one above the other. When at length it has escaped from under the last of the factories it has a level and unmolested passage to the sea, a mere *waste water*, as it were, bearing little with it but its fame; its pleasant course revealed by the morning fog which hangs over it, and the sails of the few small vessels which transact the commerce of Haverhill and Newburyport. But its real vessels are railroad cars, and its true and main stream, flowing by an iron channel further south, may be traced by a long line of vapor amid the hills, which no morning wind ever disperses, to where it empties into the sea at Boston. This side is the louder murmur now. Instead of the scream of a fish-hawk scaring the fishes, is heard the whistle of the steam-engine arousing a country to its progress.

"Sunday," *A Week on the Concord
and Merrimack Rivers,* 86–87

Roses Do Not Atone

As I walk through these old deserted wild orchards, half pasture half huckleberry field — the air is filled with fragrance from I know not what source — How much purer & sweeter it must be than the atmosphre of the streets rendered impure by the filth about our houses — It is quite offensive often when the air is heavy at night. The roses in the front yard do not atone for the sink & pig stye — & cowyard & jakes in the rear.

23 June 1852, *Journal* 5: 126

Up Goes the Smoke

When I see the smoke curling up through the woods from some farmhouse invisible — it is more suggestive of the poetry of rural and domestic life than a nearer inspection can be. — Up goes the smoke as quietly as the dew exhales in vapor from these pine leaves and oaks — as busily disposing itself in circles — and in wreathes as the housewife on the hearth below — It is cotemporary with a piece of human biography — and waves as a feather in some *man's* cap — Under that rod of sky there is some plot a-brewing — some ingenuity has planted itself, and we shall see what it will do — It tattles of more things than the boiling of the pot.

15 November 1841, *Journal* 1: 345

Immigrants

I am well enough situated here to observe one aspect of the modern world at least — I mean the migratory — the western movement. Sixteen hundred imigrants arrived at quarantine ground on the fourth of July, and more or less every day since I have been here. I see them occasionally washing their persons and clothes, or men women and children gathered on an isolated quay near the shore, stretching their limbs and taking the air, the children running races and swinging — on their artificial piece of the land of the liberty — while the vessels are undergoing purification. They are detained but a day or two, and then go up to the city, for the most part without having *landed* here.

21 July 1843, Letter to Helen Thoreau from
Staten Island, *Correspondence*, 128

I have crossed the bay 20 or 30 times and have seen a great many immigrants going up to the city for the first time—Norwegians who carry their old fashioned farming tools to the west with them, and will buy nothing here for fear of being cheated. —English operatives, known by their pale faces and stained hands, who will recover their birth-rights in a little cheap sun and wind,— English travellers on their way to the Astor House, to whom I have done the honors of the city. —Whole families of imigrants cooking their dinner upon the pavements, all sun-burnt—so that you are in doubt where the foreigner's face of flesh begins—their tidy clothes laid on, and then tied to their swathed bodies which move about like a bandaged finger—caps set on the head, as if woven of the hair, which is still growing at the roots—each and all busily cooking, stooping from time to time over the pot, and having something to drop into it, that so they may be entitled to take something out, forsooth. They look like respectable but straightened people, who may turn out to be counts when they get to Wisconsin—and will have their experience to relate to their children.

1 October 1843, Letter to Mrs. John Thoreau
from Staten Island, *Correspondence,* 141–42

Everlasting Roads

The Price Farm Road—one of those everlasting roads—which the sun delights to shine along in an August afternoon—playing truant—Which seem to stretch themselves with terrene jest as the weary traveller journeys—Where there are three white sandy furrows, two for the wheels & one between them for the horse—with endless green grass borders between—& room on each side for huckleberries & birches. — where the walls indulge in peaks — not always parallel to the ruts — & golden rod yellows all the path — Which some elms began to fringe once but left off in despair it was so long. From no point on which can you be said to be at any definite distance from a town.

23 August 1851, *Journal* 4: 11

The Boundaries of Towns

3 Pm. to Cliffs via Bear Hill. As I go through the fields endeavoring to recover my tone & sanity — & to perceive things truly & simply again, after having been perambulating the bounds of the town all the week, and dealing with the most common place and worldly minded men, and emphatically *trivial* things I feel as if I had committed suicide in a sense. I am again forcibly struck with the truth of the fable of Apollo serving king Admetus — its universal applicability. A fatal coarseness is the result of mixing in the trivial affairs of men. Though I have been associating even with the *select* men of this and the surrounding towns, I feel inexpressibly begrimmed, my pegasus has lost his wings, he has turned a reptile and gone on his belly. Such things are compatible only with a cheap and superficial life

The poet must keep himself unstained and aloof. Let him perambulate the bounds of Imagination's provinces the realms of faery, and not the insignificant boundaries of towns. The excursions of the imagination are so boundless — the limits of towns are so petty.

20 September 1851, *Journal* 4: 84–85

Crowds of Men

A crowd of men seem to generate vermin even of the human kind. In great towns there is degradation undreamed of elsewhere, — gamblers, dog-killers, rag-pickers. Some live by robbery or luck. There was the Concord muster (of last September). I see still a well-dressed man carefully and methodically searching for money on the muster-fields, far off across the river. I turn my glass upon him and notice how he proceeds. (I saw them searching there in the fall till the snow came.) He walks regularly and slowly back and forth over the ground where the soldiers had their tents, — still marked by the straw, — with his head prone, and poking in the straw with a stick, now and then turning back or aside to examine something more closely. He is dressed, methinks, better than an average man whom you meet on the streets. How can he pay for his board thus? He dreams of finding a few coppers, or perchance a half-dime, which have fallen from the soldiers' pockets, and no doubt he *will* find something of the kind, having dreamed of it, — having knocked, this door will be opened to him.

2 May 1860, *Journal* XIII: 272–73

Stakes in the Ground

I have lately been surveying the Walden woods so extensively and minutely that I now see it mapped in my mind's eye — as, indeed, on paper — as so many men's wood-lots, and am aware when I walk there that I am at a given moment passing from such a one's wood-lot to such another's. I fear this particular dry knowledge may affect my imagination and fancy, that it will not be easy to see so much wildness and native vigor there as formerly. No thicket will seem so unexplored now that I know that a stake and stones may be found in it. In these respects those Maine woods differed essentially from ours. There you are never reminded that the wilderness which you are threading is, after all, some villager's familiar wood-lot from which his ancestors have sledded their fuel for generations, or some widow's thirds, minutely described in some old deed, which is recorded, of which the owner has got a plan, too, and old bound marks may be found every forty rods if you will search. What a history this Concord wilderness which I affect so much may have had! How many old deeds describe it, — some particular wild spot, — how it passed from Cole to Robinson, and Robinson to Jones, and Jones finally to Smith, in course of years! Some have cut it over three times during their lives, and some burned it and sowed it with rye, and built walls and made a pasture of it, perchance. All have re-newed the bounds and reblazed the trees many times. 'Tis true the map informs you that you stand on land granted by the State to such an academy, or on Bing-ham's Purchase, but these names do not impose on you, for you see nothing to remind you of the academy or of Bingham.

1 January 1858, *Journal* X: 233–34

The Butcher's Huckleberries

I hear of pickers ordered out of the huckleberry-fields, and I see stakes set up with written notices forbidding any to pick there. Some let their fields, or allow so much for the picking. *Sic transit gloria ruris.* We are not grate-ful enough that we have lived part of our lives before these evil days came. What becomes of the true value of country life? What if you must go to market for it? Shall things come to such a pass that the butcher commonly brings round huckleberries in his cart? It is as if the hangman were to perform the marriage ceremony, or were to preside at the communion table. Such is the inevitable tendency of *our* civilization, — to reduce huckleberries to a level with beef-steak. The butcher's item on the door is now "calf's head and huckleberries." I suspect that the inhabitants of England and of the Continent of Europe have thus lost their natural rights with the increase of population and of monopolies. The wild fruits of the earth disappear before civilization, or are only to be found in large markets. The whole country becomes, as it were, a town or beaten common, and the fruits left are a few hips and haws.

6 August 1858, *Journal* XI: 78–79

A Convention of Men

In obedience to an instinct of their nature men have pitched their cabins, and planted corn and potatoes within speaking distance of one another, and so formed towns and villages, but they have not associated, they have only assembled, and society has signified only a *convention* of men.

14 March 1838, *Journal* 1: 38

A Sort of Harmony:
The Village and a Sense of Place

Thoreau had mellowed with the years. He found time to stop and gossip with his townsmen on his daily journey to the post office. . . . When Sam Staples bought property adjacent to Emerson's that spring [1860], he asked Thoreau to survey it. Thoreau discovered to his amusement that Emerson's boundary hedge was several feet over on Staples's property. Calling the two men together, he charged that Emerson's appropriation of the land had been intentional, only Staples had been too sharp to be imposed upon. He declared that Emerson had for years been holding up his nose as an upright citizen and an example to everybody, yet every time he reset his fence, he shoved it a little further onto Staples's property until he had stolen enough land to feed a yearling heifer. Although it was an awful disappointment to him, he said, he was glad to have a hand in exposing his dishonesty. Thoreau shouted loud enough to be heard out on the road and Emerson looked as though he had been caught picking pockets at town meeting. Staples was so embarrassed that he stared at the floor. When Thoreau made one of his harshest charges, Staples looked up, and when he saw Thoreau's eye twinkling, he let out a laugh that could be heard across town and Emerson at last realized Thoreau had been pulling his leg. The boundary "dispute," needless to say, was quickly settled amicably.

—Walter Harding

The Village

After hoeing, or perhaps reading and writing, in the forenoon, I usually bathed again in the pond, swimming across one of its coves for a stint, and washed the dust of labor from my person, or smoothed out the last wrinkle which study had made, and for the afternoon was absolutely free. Every day or two I strolled to the village to hear some of the gossip which is incessantly going on there, circulating either from mouth to mouth, or from newspaper to newspaper, and which, taken in homeopathic doses, was really as refreshing in its way as the rustle of leaves and the peeping of frogs. As I walked in the woods to see the birds and squirrels, so I walked in the village to see the men and boys; instead of the wind among the pines I heard the carts rattle. In one direction from my house there was a colony of muskrats in the river meadows; under the grove of elms and buttonwoods in the other horizon was a village of busy men, as curious to me as if they had been prairie dogs, each sitting at the mouth of its burrow, or running over to a neighbor's to gossip. I went there frequently to observe their habits. The village appeared to me a great news room; and on one side, to support it, as one at Redding & Company's on State Street, they kept nuts and raisins, or salt and meal and other groceries. Some have such a vast appetite for the former commodity, that is, the news, and such sound digestive organs, that they can sit forever in public avenues without stirring, and let it simmer and whisper through them like the Etesian winds, or as if inhaling ether, it only producing numbness and insensibility to pain, — otherwise it would often be painful to hear, — without affecting the consciousness. I hardly ever failed, when I rambled through the village, to see a row of such worthies, either sitting on a ladder sunning themselves, with their bodies inclined forward and their eyes glancing along the line this way and that, from time to time, with a voluptuous expression, or else leaning against a barn with their hands in their pockets, like caryatides, as if to prop it up. They, being commonly out of doors, heard whatever was in the wind. These are the coarsest mills, in which all gossip is first rudely digested or cracked up before it is emptied into finer and more delicate hoppers within doors. I observed that the vitals of the village were the grocery, the bar-room, the post-office, and the bank; and, as a necessary part of the machinery, they kept a bell, a big gun, and a fire-engine, at convenient places; and the houses were so arranged as to make the most of mankind, in lanes and fronting one another, so that every traveller had to run the gantlet, and every man, woman, and child might get a lick at him. Of course, those who were stationed nearest to the head of the line, where they could most see and be seen, and have the first blow at him, paid the highest prices for their places; and the few straggling inhabitants in the outskirts, where long gaps in the line began to occur, and the traveller could get over walls or turn aside into cow paths, and so escape, paid a very slight ground or window tax. Signs were hung out on all sides to allure him; some to catch him by the appetite, as the tavern and victualling cellar; some by the fancy, as the dry goods store and the jeweller's; and others by the hair or the feet or the skirts, as the barber, the shoemaker, or the tailor. Besides, there was a still more terrible standing invitation to call at every one of these houses, and company expected about these times. For the most part I escaped wonderfully from these dan-

gers, either by proceeding at once boldly and without de-
liberation to the goal, as is recommended to those who
run the gantlet, or by keeping my thoughts on high
things, like Orpheus, who, "loudly singing the praises of
the gods to his lyre, drowned the voices of the Sirens, and
kept out of danger." Sometimes I bolted suddenly, and
nobody could tell my whereabouts, for I did not stand
much about gracefulness, and never hesitated at a gap in
a fence. I was even accustomed to make an irruption into
some houses, where I was well entertained, and after
learning the kernels and very last sieve-ful of news, what
had subsided, the prospects of war and peace, and
whether the world was likely to hold together much
longer, I was let out through the rear avenues, and so escaped to the woods again.

"The Village," *Walden,* 167–69

The Fountainhead

It is apparent enough to me that only one or two of my
townsmen or acquaintances (not more than one in many
thousand men in deed—) feel or at least obey any strong
attraction drawing them toward the forest or to nature,
but all almost without exception gravitate exclusively toward men or society. The young men of Concord and in
other towns do not walk in the woods but congregate in
shops & offices— They suck one another— Their
strongest attraction is toward the mill dam.

A thousand assemble about the fountain in the public
square—the town pump—be it full or dry clear or tur-
bid, every morning but not—one in a thousand is in the
meanwhile drinking at that fountain's head.

9 February 1851, *Journal* 3: 186

A Village of Prairie Dogs

I have been into a village and there was not a man of a large soul in it— In what respect was it better than a village of prairie dogs?

9 June 1850, *Journal* 3: 84

The Boy's Water Mill

I sometimes discovered a miniature water wheel—a saw or grist mill—where the whole volume of water in some tiny rill was conducted through a junk bottle in at the open bottom & out at the nose—where some county boy whose house was not easy to be seen—some arkwright or Rennie was making his first essay in mechanics— some little trip hammer in operation mimicking the regular din of a factory—where the wild weeds & huckleberry bushes hang unmolested over the stream as the pines still do at Manchester and Lawrence— It was the work of a fabulous, farmer boy such as I never saw To come upon such unquestionable traces of a boy when I doubted if any were lingering still in this vicinity, as when you discover the trail of an otter.

One Sunday afternoon in march when the earth which had once been bared was again covered with a few inches of snow rapidly melting in the sun, as I was walking in a retired cross road away from the town, at a distance from any farm house—I heard suddenly wafted over the meadow a faint tink-tink, tink-tink, as of a cow bell amidst the birches & huckle berry bushes, but I considered that it was quite too early in the season for cows to be turned out to pasture the ground being covered with snow & it was not time to think of new-butter—and the cow bells were all safely put away in the cupboard or the till of a chest in the farm chamber. — It made me think of the days when I went huckleberrying a long time ago & heard the distant tinkling of some cows bell who was not yet mired in the swamp — from association I know of no more sweet & wild sound than this piece of copper yields, though it may not be compounded with much art Well still the sound came over the meadow louder & louder as I walked on — tink tink tink too regular for a cowbell — and I conjectured that it was a man drilling a hole in a rock — and this was the sound of his sledge on the drill —, but it was Sunday and what Concord farmer could be drilling stone! I referred the mystery to the woods beyond the meadow where alone as I thought it could be concealed — and began to think it was produced by some owl or other bird under peculiar circumstances — So getting over the fence I directed my steps through the meadow toward the wood.

But as I advanced, the sound seemed gradually to sink into the earth, while it grew louder & louder till finally it proceeded from the open meadow ground itself — and I thought of muskrats — minks & otters & expected to make a discovery in natural history — I stepped eagerly over the quaking ground — a peeping hyla & there in a little rill not more than a foot wide but as deep as wide swolen by the melting snows was a small water mill and at each revolution the wheel its crank raised a small hammer which as often fell on a tongueless cowbell which was nailed down on a board — A loud tinkling gurgle as of water leaking out of the meadow — The little rill itself seemed delighted with the din & rushed over the miniature dam & fell on the water wheel eagerly as if delighted at & proud of this loud tinkling, fast by a pilgrim's cup

the bell all spattered with mist from the fall above, &
when I had walked half a mile away a favorable wind
wafted to me in a hollow among the hills — its faint tink-
tink-tink-tink Just a fortnight after — when a new snow
had fallen, I walked near enough to this meadow to hear
the steady tink tink from the water wheel away there in
the outskirts of the town — & what is stranger than all
that very evening when I came home from a neighbors
through the village far in the night — to my astonishment
I heard from far over the meadows toward the woods
more than a mile off in a direct line the distinct tink tink
tink of trip hammer — And I called the family to the window in the village to hear the sound of the boys trip hammer in nut meadow brook — a distant & solitary place
which most of them had never seen — & they all heard it
distinctly, even some old ears which ordinarily could not
hear the birds sing — and were greatly astonished —
which I had told them of a fortnight before as of a thing
far away The sound was wafted over the water for the
meadows were flooded, a pec. state or atmosphere

Before I had thought how unlike this to all the village
sounds how remote from them as the tinkling of the rill
itself — as the golden age — the village boys know not of it
It lies far back in the outskirting meadows as the first in-
vention of the water mill in history — & now this evening
it was the one sound which possessed all the village street
— & no doubt many a villager heard it but knew not from
what remoteness as of antiquity it proceeded — borne on
the breeze gale of time from a simpler age When the
sound of every artisan was hushed — no flail no tinkling
anvil was heard — There was the still spring night — the
slumbering village & for all sound the boy's water wheel

— In a remote walk a mile & a half by the road — & a straight line one mile distant over the water — the meadows being over flown.

After 1 April 1850, Journal 3: 49–51

The Old Coat I Wear Is Concord

I am so wedded to my way of spending a day — require such broad margins of leisure, and such a complete ward-robe of old clothes, that I am ill-fitted for going abroad. Pleasant is it sometimes to sit, at home, on a single egg all day, in your own nest, though it may prove at last to be an egg of chalk. The old coat that I wear is Concord — it is my morning robe & study gown, my working dress and suit of ceremony, and my night-gown after all. Cleave to the simplest ever-Home — home — home.

27 September 1855, Letter to Daniel Ricketson,
Correspondence, 386

Letter to Emerson

Dear Friend,

Mrs. Emerson is in Boston whither she went with Eddy yesterday Saturday, and I do not know that my news will be worth sending alone. Perhaps she will come home in season to send with me from Concord. The Steam mill was burnt last night — it was a fine sight lighting up the rivers and meadows. The owners who bought it the other day for seven thousand dollars, though it was indeed insured for six, I hear since will be gainers rather than losers — but some individuals who hired of them have lost — my Father probably more than any — from four to five hundred dollars, not being insured. Some think that it was set on fire. I have no doubt that the wise fates did set it on fire, I quite agree with them that that disgrace to Concord enterprise & skill needed to be burnt away. It was a real purification as far as it went, and evidence of it was come to every man's door. I picked up cinders *in your yard* this morning 6 inches long— though there was no wind.

Your trees are doing very well; but one died in the winter—the Watson pear, a native, which apparently grew more than any other lst year, and hence it died. I am a constant foe to the caterpillars.

Mr. Alcott recommended work on the Arbor yesterday, or rather commenced repairs— But enough of this

Mr. [Cyrus] Warren tells me that he is on the point of buying the hill field for you perhaps for a hundred dollars, and he remembers that you would allow him and [Cyrus?] Stow the privilege of a *way* to their fields— I should beware how I suffered him to transact this business with such an implied privilege for his compensation. It would certainly greatly reduce the value of the field to you.

Your island wood was severely burnt—but Reuben Brown say[s] that it may stand till winter without harm before it is cut. He suffered his own to stand last year. There are applications for the Walden field and house which await your attention when you come home.

21 May 1848, Letter to Ralph Waldo Emerson,
Correspondence, 225–26

Still Related to Men

I sometimes reproach myself because I do not find anything attractive in certain more trivial employments of men—that I skip men so commonly & their affairs—the professions and the trades — do not elevate them at least in my thought and get some material for poetry out of them directly. I will not avoid then to go by where these men are repairing the Stone Bridge — see if I cannot see poetry in that — if that will not yield me a reflection. It is narrow to be confined to woods & fields and grand aspects of nature only. — The greatest & wisest will still be related to men.

23 August 1851, Journal 4: 10

These Coney Island Breakers

I am seven and a half miles from New York, and, as it would take half a day at least, have not been there yet. I have already run over no small part of the island, to the highest hill, and some way along the shore. From the hill directly behind the house I can see New York, Brooklyn, Long Island, the Narrows, through which vessels bound to and from all parts of the world chiefly pass, — Sandy Hook and the Highlands of Neversink (part of the coast of New Jersey) — and, by going still farther up the hill, the Kill van Kull, and Newark Bay. From the pinnacle of one Madame Grimes' house the other night at sunset, I could see almost round the island. Far in the horizon there was a fleet of sloops bound up the Hudson, which seemed to be going over the edge of the earth; and in view of these trading ships, commerce seems quite imposing.

But it is rather derogatory that your dwelling-place should be only a neighborhood to a great city, — to live on an inclined plane. I do not like their cities and forts, with their morning and evening guns, and sails flapping in one's eye. I want a whole continent to breathe in, and a good deal of solitude and silence, such as all Wall Street

cannot buy,—nor Broadway with its wooden pavement.
I must live along the beach, on the southern shore, which
looks directly out to sea,—and see what that great pa-
rade of water means, that dashes and roars, and has not
yet wet me, as long as I have lived.

I must not know anything about my condition and relations here till what is not permanent is worn off. I have
not yet subsided. Give me time enough and I may like it.
All my inner man heretofore has been a Concord impression; and here come these Sandy Hook and Coney Island breakers to meet and modify the former; but it will
be long before I can make nature look as innocently
grand and inspiring as in Concord.

Your affectionate son,

Henry D. Thoreau.

11 May 1843, Letter to Mrs. John Thoreau,
Correspondence, 99–100

Through a Traveller's Eyes

When you are starting away—leaving your more familiar
fields for a little adventure like a walk—you look at every
object with a travellers or at least with historical eyes—
you pause on the first bridge.

—where an ordinary walk hardly commences, & begin to observe & moralize like a traveller—It is worthe
the while to see your native Village thus sometimes—as
if you were a traveller passing through it—commenting
on your neighbors as strangers.

4 September 1851, *Journal* 4: 37

Secure Us a Culture

There are certain refining & civilizing influences as
works of art—journals—& books & scientific instru-

ments — which this community is amply rich enough to purchase which would educate this village — elevate its tone of thought, & if it alone improved these opportunities easily make it the centre of civilization in the known world — put us on a level as to opportunities at once with London & Arcadia — and secure us a culture at once superior to both — Yet we spend 16000 dollars on a Town House a hall for our political meetings mainly — and nothing to educate ourselves who are grown up. Pray is there nothing in the market — no advantages — no intellectual food worth buying? Have Paris & London & New York & Boston nothing to dispose of which this Village might buy & appropriate to its own use. Might not this great villager adorn his villa with a few pictures & statues — enrich himself with a choice library as available without being cumbrous as any in the world — with scientific instruments for such as have a taste to use them. Yet we are contented to be countrified — to be provincial. I am astonished to find that in this 19th century — in this land of free schools — we spend absolutely nothing as a town on our own education cultivation civilization. Each town like each individual has its own character — some more some less cultivated. I know many towns so mean spirited & benighted that it would be a disgrace to belong to them. I believe that some of our New England villages within 30 miles of Boston are as boorish & barbarous communities as there are on the face of the earth — and how much superior are the best of them? If London has any refinement any information to sell why should we not buy it?

27 September 1851, *Journal* 4: 102–3

Content to Be in Concord

I am chiefly indebted to your letters for what I have learned of Concord and family news, and am very glad when I get one. I should have liked to be in Walden woods with you, but not with the railroad. I think of you all very often, and wonder if you are still separated from me only by so many miles of earth, or so many miles of memory. This life we live is a strange dream, and I don't believe at all any account men give of it. Methinks I should be content to sit at the back-door in Concord, under the poplar tree, henceforth forever. Not that I am homesick at all, — for places are strangely indifferent to me, — but Concord is still a cynosure to my eyes, and I find it hard to attach it, even in imagination, to the rest of the globe, and tell where the seam is.

6 August 1843, Letter to Mrs. John Thoreau,
Correspondence, 131

A Warm Night

A warm night like this at this season produces its effect on the village — The boys are heard at play in the street now at 9 o'clock — in greater force & with more noise than usual. My neighbor has got out his flute — There is more fog than usual — the moon is full. The tops of the woods in the horizon seen above the fog look exactly like long low black clouds — the fog being the color of the sky.

8 October 1851, *Journal* 4: 134

All Degrees of Barbarism

When I think of the Carlisle man whom I saw today — & the filthiness of his house — I am reminded that there are all degrees of barbarism even in this so called civilized community. Carlisle too belongs to the 19th century.

13 December 1851, *Journal* 4: 204

Bill Wheeler

Bill Wheeler—he had two clumps for feet and progressed slowly by short steps—having frozen his feet once as I understood. Him I have been sure to meet once in five years progressing into the town—on his stubs holding the middle of the road—out of what confines—whose hired man having been—(especially on a military day) I never knew— In what remote barn having quartered all these years— He seemed to belong to a different caste from other men—and reminded me of both the Indian Pariah & martyr— I understood that somebody was found to give him his drink—for the few chores he could do— I never heard any mention of his meat whether he had or wanted any. One day since this, not long ago—I saw in my walk a kind of shelter such as woodmen might use in the woods by the Great Meadows made of meadow hay cast over a rude frame— Thrusting my head in at a hole as I am wont to do in such cases—I found Bill Wheeler there curled up asleep on the hay who being suddenly awakened from a sound sleep rubbed his eyes & inquired if I found any game thinking I was sporting. I came away reflecting much on that man's life— How he communicated with none—how now perchance he did chores for none— How low he lived perhaps from a deep principle—that he might be some mighty philosopher greater than Socrates or Diogenes—simplifying life—returning to nature—having turned his back on towns— How many things he had put off—luxuries—comforts—human society even in his feet—wrestling with his thoughts I felt even as Diogenes when he saw the boy drinking out of his hands — & threw away his cup. Here was one who went alone — did no work & had no relatives that I knew of — was not ambitious that I could see — did not depend on the good opinion of men. Must he not see things with an impartial eye — disinterested as a toad observes the gardener! Perchance here is one of a sect of philosophers — the only one — so simple — so abstracted in thought & life from his contemporaries — That his wisdom is indeed foolishness to them. Who knows but in his solitary meadow-hay bunk he indulges in thought only in triumphant satires on men — Who knows but here is a superiority to literature unexpressed & inexpressible! Who has resolved to humble and mortify himself as never man was humbled & mortified — Whose very vividness of perception — clear knowledge & insight have made him dumb — leaving no common consciousness & ground of parlance with his kind — or rather his unlike kindred! Whose news plainly is not my news nor yours. I was not sure for a moment but here was a philosopher who had left far behind him the philosophers of Greece & India — & I envied him his advantageous point of view.

16 January 1852, *Journal* 4: 258–60

Sudbury Haines

Met Sudbury Haines on the river before the Cliffs come a fishing. Wearing an old coat much patched with many colors. He represents the Indian still. The very patches in his coat and his improvident life do so — I feel that he is as essential a part nevertheless of our community as the lawyer in the village.

9 February 1852, *Journal* 4: 337–38

The Village Church

The moonlight is the best restorer of antiquity— The houses in the village have a classical elegance as of the best days of Greece—and this half finished church reminds me of the Parthenon, or whatever is most famous and excellent in art. So serene it stands reflecting the moon, and intercepting the stars with its rafters, as if it were refreshed by the dews of the night equally with me.

3 September 1841, *Journal* 1: 329

I was once reproved by a minister who was driving a poor beast to some meeting-house horse-sheds among the hills of New Hampshire, because I was bending my steps to a mountain-top on the Sabbath, instead of a church, when I would have gone further than he to hear a true word spoken on that or any day. He declared that I was "breaking the Lord's fourth commandment," and proceeded to enumerate, in a sepulchral tone, the disasters which had befallen him whenever he had done any ordinary work on the Sabbath. He really thought that a god was on the watch to trip up those men who followed any secular work on this day, and did not see that it was the evil conscience of the workers that did it. The country is full of this superstition, so that when one enters a village, the church, not only really but from association, is the ugliest looking building in it, because it is the one in which human nature stoops the lowest and is most disgraced.

"Sunday," *A Week on the Concord
and Merrimack Rivers*, 75–76

Village Bells

Sat. 18th 1841. Barn

It is a great event — the hearing of a bell ring in one of the neighboring towns — particularly in the night. It excites in me an unusual hilarity — and I feel that I am in season wholly — and enjoy a prime and leisure hour.

18 September 1841, *Journal* 1: 333

In this stillness & at this distance I hear the 9 o'clock bell in Bedford 5 miles off — which I might never hear in the village but here its music surmounts the village din — and has something very sweet & noble & inspiring in it, associated in part with the hooting of owls.

21 January 1853, *Journal* 5: 449

A Poem Called Concord

I think I could write a poem to be called Concord — For argument I should have the River — the Woods — the Ponds — the Hills — the Fields — the Swamps and Meadows — the Streets and Buildings — and the Villagers. Then Morning — Noon — and Evening — Spring Summer — Autumn and Winter — Night — Indian Summer — and the Mountains in the Horizon.

4 September 1841, *Journal* 1: 330

My Mate, the Canal Builder

I have been making pencils all day — and then at evening walked to see an old — schoolmate who is going to help make the Welland canal navigable for ships round Niagara. —

He cannot see any such motives and modes of living as I — Professes not to look beyond the securing of certain "Creature comforts." And so we go silently different ways

—with all serenity—I in the still moon light through the village this fair evening to write these thoughts in my journal—and he forsooth to mature his schemes to ends as good maybe but different.

17 March 1842, Journal 1: 379

Haden's Labor, My Labor

Just after sunrise this morning I noticed Haden walking beside his team which was slowly drawing a heavy hewn stone swung under the axle—surrounded by an atmosphere of industry. His days work begun— Honest peaceful industry—conserving the world—which all men—respect—which society has consecrated. A reproach to all sluggards & idlers. Pausing abreast the shoulders of his oxen & half turning round with a flourish of his merciful whip while they gained their length on him. And I thought such is the labor which the American congress exists to protect—honest manly toil— His brow has commenced to sweat. Honest as the day is long. One of the sacred band doing the needful but irksome drudgery. Toil that makes his bread taste sweet & keeps society sweet. The day went by and at evening I passed a rich man's yard who keeps many servants and foolishly spends much money while he adds nothing to the common stock. And there I saw Haden's stone lying beside a whimsical structure intended to adorn this Lord Timothy Dexter's mansion—and the dignity forthwith departed from Haden's labor—in my eyes— I am frequently invited to survey farms in a rude manner a very and insignificant labor—though I manage to get more out of it than my employers—but I am never invited by the community to do anything quite worth the while to do. The industry of the boor traced to the end is found to be subserving some rich man's foolish enterprise. There is a coarse boisterous money-making fellow—in the N part of the town who is going to build a bank wall under the hill along the edge of his meadow—the powers have put this into his head to keep him out of mischief—and he wishes me to spend three weeks digging there with him— The result will be that he will perchance get a little more money to hoard or leave for his heirs to spend foolishly when he is dead— Now if I do this the community will commend me as an industrious & hard-working man—but as I choose to devote myself to labors which yield more real profit though but little money they regard me as a loafer— But as I do not need this police of meaningless labor to regulate me and do not see any thing absolutely praiseworthy in his undertaking however amusing it may be to him, I prefer to finish my education at a different school.

24 July 1852, *Journal* 5: 244–45

Evening in the Village

The streets of the village are much more interesting to me at this hour of a summer evening than by day. Neighbors and also farmers come ashopping after their day's haying are chatting in the streets and I hear the sound of many musical instruments and of singing from various houses. For a short hour or two the inhabitants are sensibly employed.

21 July 1851, *Journal* 3: 325

I Thank My Stars for Melvin

Got in my boat, which before I had got out and turned up on the bank. It made me sweat to wheel it home through the snow, I am so unused to the work of late.

Then walked up the railroad. The clear straw-colored grass and some weeds contrasting with the snow it rises above. Saw little in this walk. Saw Melvin's lank bluish-white-black-spotted hound, and Melvin with his gun near, going home at eve. He follows hunting, praise be to him, as regularly in our tame fields as the farmers follow farming. Persistent Genius! How I respect and thank him for him! I trust the Lord will provide us with another Melvin when he is gone. How good in him to follow his own bent, and not continue at the Sabbath-school all his days! What a wealth he thus becomes in the neighborhood! Few know how to take the census. I thank my stars for Melvin. I think of him with gratitude when I am going to sleep, grateful that he exists, — that Melvin who is such a trial to his mother. Yet he is agreeable to me as a tinge of russet on the hillside. I would fain give thanks morning and evening for my blessings. Awkward, gawky, loose-hung, dragging his legs after him. He is my contemporary and neighbor. He is one tribe, I am another, and we are not at war.

2 December 1856, *Journal* IX: 148

The Trees of the Village

No annual training or muster of soldiery, no celebration with its scarfs and banners, could import into the town a hundredth part of the annual splendor of our October. We have only to set the trees, or let them stand, and Nature will find the colored drapery, — flags of all her nations, some of whose private signals hardly the botanist can read. Let us have a good many maples and hickories and scarlet oaks, then, I say. Blaze away! Shall that dirty roll of bunting in the gunhouse be all the colors a village can display? A village is not complete unless it has these trees to mark the season in it. They are as important as a town clock. Such a village will not be found to work well. It has a screw loose; an essential part is wanting. Let us have willows for spring, elms for summer, maples and walnuts and tupelos for autumn, evergreens for winter, and oaks for all seasons. What is a gallery in a house to a gallery in the streets! I think that there is not a picture gallery in the country which would be worth so much to us as is the western view under the elms of our main street.

18 October 1858, *Journal* XI: 220

Father's Village

As far as I know, Father, when he died, was not only one of the oldest men in the middle of Concord, but the one perhaps best acquainted with the inhabitants, and the local, social, and street history of the middle of the town, for the last fifty years. He belonged in a peculiar sense to the village street; loved to sit in the shops or at the post-office and read the daily papers. I think that he remembered more about the worthies (and unworthies) of Concord village forty years ago, both from dealing as a trader and from familiar intercourse with them, than any one else. Our other neighbors, now living or very recently dead, have either come to the town more recently than he, or have lived more aloof from the mass of the inhabitants.

3 February 1859, *Journal* XI: 436–37

Brother's Flute

I have heard my brother playing on his flute at evening half a mile off through the houses of the village every note with perfect distinctness— It seemed a more beautiful communication with me than the sending up of a rocket would have been.

12 May 1850, *Journal* 3: 68

Mother's Memories

My mother was telling to-night of the sounds which she used to hear summer nights when she was young and lived on the Virginia Road,—the lowing of cows, or cackling of geese, or the beating of a drum as far off as Hildreth's, but above all Joe Merriam whistling to his team, for he was an admirable whistler. Says she used to get up at midnight and go and sit on the door-step when all in the house were asleep, and she could hear nothing in the world but the ticking of the clock in the house behind her.

26 May 1857, *Journal* IX: 381

Editor's Note

The passages contained in this volume represent but a small sample of Thoreau's writings about the land. The chapters are loosely organized chronologically, to provide selections of Thoreau's thoughts on the evolution of the Concord landscape from the time when it was inhabited by Native Americans through the early years of Thoreau's life, when the area was largely agricultural, to a period when the railroad brought growth and change to Concord's village and surrounding countryside. Interspersed are chapters with selections that show Thoreau's ideas on conservation and his belief in the importance of undisturbed land to the growth of the human spirit.

The passages were selected with the hope of providing the reader with additional insight into the inner life of a man who, in simply wishing "to speak a word for nature," changed the way we relate to our world today. I have tried to include selections that demonstrate Thoreau's range of emotion — not only his passion and poetry, but his wit and humor as well. Some of the passages will be familiar, but I think many will be refreshing and surprising.

Most of the selections are taken from Thoreau's journal, which was the primary source of inspiration for his other works. Here one finds the raw material of his philosophy and ideas, not yet shaped by editors with a reading public in mind. The journal is often more personal than his other works, enabling the reader to get to know him better. As Thoreau himself wrote:

> I do not know but thoughts written down thus in a journal might be printed in the same Form with greater advantage — than if the related ones were brought together into separate essays. They are now allied to life — & are seen by the reader not to be far fetched — It is more simple — less artful — I feel that in the other case I should have no proper frame for my sketches. Mere facts & names & dates communicate more than we suspect — Whether the flower looks better in the nosegay — than in the meadow where it grew — & we had to wet our feet to get it! Is the scholastic air any advantage?

For nearly a century the standard edition of Thoreau's works has been *The Writings of Henry David Thoreau,* edited by Bradford Torrey and Francis H. Allen, 20 volumes (Boston: Houghton Mifflin, 1906), volumes VII to XX of which comprise the *Journal* (separately numbered I to XIV). The 1906 Houghton Mifflin edition is being superseded by the ongoing *The Writings of Henry D. Thoreau* (Princeton, N.J.: Princeton University Press, 1971–), which among other titles has published five volumes of the *Journal* to date. The Princeton edition of the *Journal* prints Thoreau's text exactly as it appears in manuscript and retains all peculiarities of his spelling, punctuation, and syntax. In "The Spirit of Thoreau" series, arabic numerals indicate the five volumes of the Princeton edition; roman numerals, the volumes of the 1906 *Journal* not yet superseded by Princeton.

Further Reading

Works by Thoreau

The Correspondence of Henry David Thoreau. Edited by Walter Harding and Carl Bode. New York: New York University Press, 1958.

Early Essays and Miscellanies. Edited by Joseph Muldenhaur and Edwin Moser, with Alexander Kern. Princeton University Press, 1975.

The Maine Woods. Edited by Joseph J. Moldenhauer. Princeton: Princeton University Press, 1972.

Walden. Edited by J. Lyndon Shanley. Princeton: Princeton University Press, 1971

"Walking." In *The Natural History Essays.* Introduction and Notes by Robert Sattelmeyer. Salt Lake City: Peregrine Smith, 1980.

A Week on the Concord and Merrimack Rivers. Edited by Carl F. Hovde, William Howarth, and Elizabeth Hall Witherell. Princeton: Princeton University Press, 1980.

Other Works Cited

Allen, Francis H., ed. *Men of Concord: And Some Others As Portrayed in the Journal of Henry David Thoreau.* Boston: Houghton Mifflin, 1936.

Anderson, Charles R., ed. *Thoreau's World: Miniatures from His Journal.* Englewood Cliffs, N.J.: Prentice Hall, 1971.

Baker, Carlos. *Emerson Among the Eccentrics: A Group Portrait.* New York: Viking, 1996.

Berry, Wendell. *Standing by Words.* San Francisco: North Point Press, 1983.

———. *The Gift of Good Land: Further Essays, Cultural and Agricultural.* San Francisco: North Point Press, 1981.

Blanding, Thomas. "A Historical Perspective." *The Concord Journal,* 21 December 1995.

Brooks, Paul. *The People of Concord.* Chester, Conn.: Globe Pequot Press, 1990.

Canby, Henry Seidel. *Thoreau.* Boston: Houghton Mifflin, 1939.

Channing, William Ellery. *Thoreau: The Poet Naturalist.* Boston: Roberts Brothers, 1873.

Cook, Reginald Lansing. *The Concord Saunterer.* Middlebury, Vt.: Middlebury College Press, 1940.

Ells, Stephen F. "Henry Thoreau and the Estabrook Country: A Historic and Personal Landscape." *Concord Saunterer* 4, new series (1996): 73–148.

Emerson, Edward Waldo. *Henry Thoreau: As Remembered by a Young Friend.* Concord, Mass.: Thoreau Foundation, 1968.

Emerson, Ralph Waldo. *Journals and Miscellaneous Notebooks.* Edited by William H. Gilman, Ralph H. Orth, and others. Cambridge, Mass.: Belknap Press/Harvard University Press, 1960–1982.

Fleck, Richard F. *Henry Thoreau and John Muir Among the Indians.* Hamden, Conn.: Archon Books, 1985.

Foster, David R. *Thoreau's Country: Journey Through a Transformed Landscape.* Cambridge, Mass.: Harvard University Press, 1999.

Gleason, Herbert W. *Thoreau Country.* San Francisco: Sierra Club Books, 1975.

Gross, Robert A. "Culture and Cultivation: Agriculture and Society in Thoreau's Concord." *Journal of American History* 69, no. 1 (1982): 42–61.

———. "'The Most Estimable Place in All the World': A Debate on Progress in Nineteenth-Century Concord." In *Studies in the American Renaissance.* Edited by Joel Myerson. Boston: Twayne, 1978, pp. 1–15.

Harding, Walter. *The Days of Henry Thoreau.* New York: Alfred A. Knopf, 1965.

———. *A Thoreau Handbook.* New York: New York University Press, 1959.

Harding, Walter, ed. *Thoreau: A Century of Criticism.* Dallas: Southern Methodist University Press, 1954.

Krutch, Joseph Wood. *Henry David Thoreau.* New York: William Sloane Associates, 1948.

Larkin, Jack. *The Reshaping of Everyday Life: 1790–1840.* New York: Harper & Row, 1988.

Richardson, Robert D. Jr. *Henry Thoreau: A Life of the Mind.* Berkeley: University of California Press, 1986.

Rothwell, Robert L. *Henry David Thoreau: An American Landscape.* New York: Paragon House, 1991.

Sayre, Robert F. *Thoreau and the American Indians.* Princeton: Princeton University Press, 1977.

Shi, David E. *The Simple Life: Plain Living and High Thinking in American Culture.* New York: Oxford University Press, 1985.

Zwinger, Ann, and Edwin Way Teale. *A Conscious Stillness: Two Naturalists on Thoreau's Rivers.* New York: Harper & Row, 1982.

Acknowledgments

This book is dedicated to Tasha Tudor: With generations of children by her side, she advances confidently in the direction of her dreams — daring to live the life which she has imagined.

For their helpful assistance in the research and preparation of the manuscript I would like to thank Leslie Wilson, Curator of Special Collections, and the staff at the Concord Free Public Library; and Tom Harris, Executive Director, and the staff of the Thoreau Society.

A special thanks to Helen Bowdoin, of the Thoreau Institute, for her support and encouragement over the years, and to the Emerson family for their friendship and for their willingness to share environments so well suited to the study of nature.

Every day, a piece of Thoreau country is threatened in one way or another. To the many grassroots organizations and individuals who, over the years, have sacrificed personal gain so that future generations might know the land as Thoreau did, I give thanks. To list them all would be an impossible task. But, with the sincere hope that I offend no one through error of omission, I would especially like to mention the following: For early efforts to protect Walden Woods, thanks to Mary Sherwood and Walden Forever Wild, and to Tom Blanding and the members of the Thoreau Country Conservation Alliance. For their continuing efforts to defend Walden's treasured landscape, I thank Don Henley, Kathi Anderson, and the Walden Woods Project. For succeeding in protecting Thoreau's birthplace and the Thoreau Farm from development, credit is due to Doris Smith for sounding the alarm and to the members of the Save the Thoreau Birthplace Foundation, the Thoreau Birthplace Task Force, the Thoreau Farm Trust, the Seefurth Foundation, and the Educational Collaborative of Greater Boston. Working with many local groups, Peter Forbes and the New England offices of the Trust for Public Lands has been invaluable in helping to set aside much open space. Also, over the course of many years, the Concord Land Conservation Trust has been instrumental in protecting a large portion of the Concord countryside so important to Thoreau. Thanks are also due to the Concord Historical Commission, the Concord Historic Districts Commission, the Massachusetts Historical Commission, the Society for the Preservation of New England Antiquities, The Trustees of Reservations, Historic Concord, Inc., and the National Park Service for the role they have played in protecting, restoring, and maintaining important historic ground around Concord. Thanks to Michael Kellett and RESTORE: The North Woods for extending their "protective arms" outside the boundaries of Concord to include many of the New England forests that Thoreau visited. For efforts to halt expansion into Estabrook Woods, one of Thoreau's "great tracts," we owe a debt of gratitude to many individuals, but especially Stephen Ells, Lansing Old, Ellie Bemis, Carol Dwyer, Annie Faulkner, and the many students and alumni of Middlesex School. Thanks to all the farmers in and around Concord who show pride in the region's agrarian roots, are committed to preserving a way of life, and who know that the worth of a good piece of land should never be judged by the number of single-family homes it will support. And, most important, thanks to the citizens of Concord and surrounding communities for having the foresight and determination to reject un-limited growth. Through their continuing efforts to pro-tect many beautiful acres of fields, meadows, and woods, they ensure that there will always be ample room for "the imagination of poets."

Finally, I thank Paula, Andrea, Casey, and Patty for their love, and for always being there.

THE SPIRIT OF THOREAU

"How many a man has dated a new era in his life from the reading of a book," wrote Henry David Thoreau in *Walden*. Today that book, perhaps more than any other American work, continues to provoke, inspire, and change lives all over the world, and each rereading is fresh and challenging. Yet as Thoreau's countless admirers know, there is more to the man than *Walden*. An engineer, poet, teacher, naturalist, lecturer, and political activist, he truly had several lives to lead, and each one speaks forcefully to us today.

The Spirit of Thoreau introduces the thoughts of a great writer on a variety of important topics, some that we readily associate him with, some that may be surprising. Each book includes selections from his familiar published works as well as from less well known and even previously unpublished lectures, letters, and journal entries. Thoreau claimed that "to read well, that is, to read true books in a true spirit, is a noble exercise, and one that will task the reader more than any exercise which the customs of the day esteem." The volume editors and the Thoreau Society believe that you will find these new aspects of Thoreau an exciting "exercise" indeed.

This Thoreau Society series reunites Henry Thoreau with

his historic publisher. For more than a hundred years, the venerable publishing firm of Houghton Mifflin has been associated with standard editions of the works of Emerson and Thoreau and with important bibliographical and interpretive studies of the New England transcendentalists. Until Princeton University Press began issuing new critical texts in *The Writings of Henry D. Thoreau,* beginning with *Walden* in 1971, Thoreauvians were well served by Houghton Mifflin's twenty-volume edition of *The Writings of Henry David Thoreau* (1906). Having also published Walter Harding's annotated edition of *Walden* (1995), Houghton Mifflin is again in the forefront of Thoreau studies.

You are invited to continue exploring Thoreau by joining our society. For well over fifty years we have presented publications, annual gatherings, and other programs to further the appreciation of Thoreau's thought and writings. And now we have embarked on a bold new venture. In partnership with the Walden Woods Project, the Thoreau Society has formed the Thoreau Institute, a research and educational center housing the world's greatest collection of materials by and about Thoreau. In ways that the author of *Walden* could not have imagined, his message is still changing lives in a brand-new era.

For membership information, write to the Thoreau Society, 44 Baker Farm, Lincoln, MA 01773-3004, or call 781-259-4750. To learn more about the Thoreau Institute, write to the same address; call 781-259-4700; or visit the Web site:

www.walden.org.

WESLEY T. MOTT
Series Editor
The Thoreau Society